T0113859

Searching
for
Heroes
in
Life,
Vol. 2:

What the CORONAVIRUS PANDEMIC
Tells Us about HEROES

Charles Brookins Taylor, Sr.

WESTBOW
P R E S S®
A DIVISION OF THOMAS NELSON
& ZONDERVAN

WestBow Press books may be ordered through booksellers or by contacting:

WestBow Press
A Division of Thomas Nelson & Zondervan
1663 Liberty Drive
Bloomington, IN 47403
www.westbowpress.com
844-714-3454

ISBN: 978-1-6642-6508-0 (sc)
ISBN: 978-1-6642-6507-3 (e)

Print information available on the last page.

WestBow Press rev. date: 05/24/2022

This book is dedicated to all our heroes in the past who gave so much to us, many from every walk of life today, and especially those in the midst of the coronavirus pandemic who are serving in heroic ways.

Contents

Acknowledgments

Thanks to all the many heroes in our midst, some of whom allowed me the privilege of observing and dialoguing with them and encouraged me to write this book.

Thanks also to my family members and friends, who in their own individual ways inspired me along this writing assignment.

Finally, I thank my publisher, WestBow Press, a division of Thomas Nelson and Zondervan, and their many specialists who guided me through the process of writing this book.

Introduction

I thought I had seen it all.

I thought I had seen it all. Then along came COVID-19, the coronavirus pandemic.

After graduating from high school, serving in the US Air Force as an air policeman, serving on several airbases, and serving oversea tours, I thought I had seen it all.

After graduating from college and teaching in the public school systems for nearly thirty years, I thought I had seen it all.

After raising five children and serving as pastor of several churches as a minister of the Gospel, yes, I thought I had seen it all.

And even after serving on site as an air force civil air patrol chaplain in New York City on September 12, 2001, as a result of the 9/11 terrorist attack, I thought I had seen it all.

Then along came the coronavirus pandemic. Like a thief in the night, it came unexpectedly, busting on the scene, spreading like a mighty rushing wind, and penetrating every aspect of life worldwide.

Once again, we are reminded how limited is our ultimate control over what can happen in our lives.

Why Write *Searching for Heroes in Life?*

The coronavirus pandemic has directly affected every aspect of life worldwide, more so than any other modern pandemic to date. Think about it. It has affected over two hundred countries, territories, and tribes either directly or indirectly. It is estimated that the world's population is approximately eight billion people. No population has been totally exempted.

The coronavirus reminds us that we are in a nonvoluntary war, fighting an invisible enemy who is no respecter of person; it attacks people from every walk and at every stage of life.

More than any modern event, it has highlighted heroes from every walk of life, even people who many thought were not significant or important or essential for our normal existence.

The coronavirus has awakened us from our slumbering sleep, in that we are beginning to see heroes all around us, both small and big, and many of them have gone unrecognized before. The coronavirus pandemic is teaching us more about heroes in our life than we ever knew before. Moreover, it is causing us to realize how much we depend on each other in meeting our needs.

The coronavirus pandemic presents an ideal case study for searching for heroes in life. It speaks volumes as to why we must take a fresh and deeper look at what it means to be a hero. It is helping us understand how to recognize them in every aspect of our existence. Among other things, it is showing us the many reasons why we must show a sincere gratitude for each one (which I will expound on in chapter 8).

As I pondered on this, a quiet, still voice within me prompted me over and over again to write *Searching for Heroes in Life, Vol. 2: What the Coronavirus Pandemic Tells Us about Heroes.* This prompting grew stronger day by day. My spiritual discernment told me it is a divine prompting from God. My experience has taught me it is a wise choice to obey God's prompting. And so here I am in obedience, as I stand ready to take on this task.

I invite you to join with me in this eye-opening journey. As a result, we will become more aware of and thankful for heroes in our lives that help us to meet our everyday needs. In the process, we will discover that we too are called to be heroes.

Join me on this journey.

Chapter 1

Using the Tool of Repetition

I begin with a special reminder of why I will occasionally use the powerful tool of repetition throughout this book. First of all, in a personal way, I have learned the value of using repetition as a teaching and learning tool in sports. One of the first teachers who impressed upon me the importance of repetition was my Japanese teacher (sensei) as I studied judo, a form of martial arts during my overseas duties while serving in the US Air Force. Even after I was promoted to the rank of black belt, as a student, I was required to always repeat the basic techniques before practicing the advanced techniques.

I have adopted this teaching method over the years as a coach, teacher, and trainer in martial arts and other sports.

In fact, it has been said that if you practice anything thousands upon thousands of times, over and over again, invariably you will learn to do it better. And eventually you will create what is called overlearning, a point beyond immediate recalling.

Second of all, as a teacher, I have used this method in the public school system for nearly thirty years. I have found it to be beneficial for both the slow and fast learners. So welcome to the club as we refresh our memory concerning some key points I made earlier in *Searching for Heroes in Life, Vol. 1* about heroes and why we need others to help us meet our needs in life.

Recalling Key Points I Made in *Searching for Heroes in Life, Vol. 1* about Heroes and Why We Need Them

1. A basic definition of the word *hero*: According to *The New Shorter Oxford English Dictionary, Fourth Edition,* (1993), a hero is a person recognized or admired for his or her courage, ability, or achievement and noble qualities in any field. What does it mean to recognize someone? Recognizing someone is an act of acknowledgment or admission of a service or achievement; to show appreciation of service or achievement.

2. Why we need heroes: Every human being has needs. Each one of us needs heroes in our lives to have our needs met, from the very basic to the more advanced needs.

3. The Maslow hierarchy of needs: According to Abraham Maslow's hierarchy of needs, there are five levels. Maslow moves from the basic (that is, the physiological needs) to the more complex needs. The following is a list of Maslow's five levels of needs and a brief summary of each.

(1) Physiological Needs—These needs are said to be the most basic and are vital to survival: water, air, food, and sleep. Maslow believed that all other needs become secondary until the physiological needs are met.

(2) Security Needs—These are the needs for safety and security. They are important for survival but are not as demanding as the physiological needs. Examples of security needs include a desire for steady employment, health care, safe neighborhoods, and shelter from the environment.

(3) Social Needs—These include the needs for belonging, love, and affection. Maslow described

these needs as less basic than physiological and security needs. Relationships such as friendships, romantic attachments, and families help fulfill the need for companionship and acceptance, as does involvement in social, community, or religious groups.

(4) Esteem Needs—After the first three needs are satisfied, self-esteem becomes increasingly important. These include the need for things that reflect on self-esteem, personal worth, social recognition, and a sense of accomplishment.

(5) Self-actualization Needs—This is the highest level of needs and refers to a person's full potential. Maslow describes this level as the desire to accomplish everything that one can and to become the most one can be. This level of need may focus on a personal desire. For example, a person may have the desire to be the very best athlete. Another person may have a strong desire to become an ideal parent. Another person may have the strong desire to become an ideal painter. Others may want to express their best selves in painting, writing, politics, inventions, or something else. Maslow believed that to understand this level of need, the person must not only achieve the previous needs, but master them.[1]

I believe Maslow's hierarchy of needs must be given much credence. I am sure you are aware that some people have become successful in life despite not having their basic needs met in a systematic way. However, it is my belief and experience that our highest form of life actualization is achieved by reaching the level of *spiritual self-actualization*—a sixth level of need, so to speak. This need is actualized the moment we establish a personal relationship with God, our greatest hero.

Once we reach the spiritual self-actualization level, that which is in the spiritual realm, we then have access to a level that transcends the natural realm of life. Yet, we must keep in mind that the spiritual realm can permeate and operate withing the natural realm, which includes our basic needs mentioned by Maslow.

At this juncture, some of you are aware that I am repeating some of what I said in *Searching for Heroes in Life, Vol. 1*. Remember that I am intentionally using the method of repetition for "slow learners" such as myself. So I ask you "fast learners" to be patient with us.

Heroes Can Come from Every Walk of Life

It has been said that if you believe each of us has been designed by God for a specific reason, then you will know there is no such thing as an ordinary person. Let me give a simple definition of a hero to underscore this very point. A hero is a person who does something for us or says something to us that encourages us to move forward in life. A hero uses his or her gifts to bless others.

As you read *Searching for Heroes in Life, Vol. 2: What the Coronavirus Pandemic Tells Us about Heroes*, you are going to discover how the coronavirus pandemic is highlighting a broad spectrum of heroes who many never thought were heroes before—people who help meet our daily needs, big or small, rich or poor, from every walk of life. In the process, I believe we will be moved, on an individual and collective basis, to be more grateful for the role that everyone can play in our society.

We Must Not Allow the Media and Other Components in Our Society to Set Boundaries or Establish Parameters by which We Define Heroes

I began to realize more and more each day that we humans, especially young people, are allowing the media and other components of our society to not only define who our heroes are but also establish the parameters or boundaries by which they can be defined.

As I approached my last years of teaching in the public school system, I began recognizing the importance of impressing upon my students the need to know that each one of us has the potential to become a hero by using the unique gifts that God gives each one of us.

On the first day of school, I began making it a standing policy to ask my students the following question: What do you want to be when you grow up? These were the most common answers I received from my students:

(1) "I want to be a doctor when I grow up."
(2) "I want to be a football player when I grow up."
(3) "I want to be a basketball player when I grow up."
(4) "I want to be a lawyer when I grow up."
(5) "I want to be an airplane pilot when I grow up."
(6) "I want to be a fashion designer or a model when I grow up."
(7) "I want to be an engineer when I grow up."
(8) "I want to become rich and famous when I grow up."

As I listened to these answers, it was clear I needed to encourage each student who had expressed their aspiration to become one of these persons. I did not hesitate to commend them for setting a goal in life by letting them know it would be good if they could become one of these persons. However, I was careful to remind them that they could also become heroes by excelling in other career pursuits.

As a follow-up, I would always ask a question to direct them to the point I was trying to make: "Class, I want you to think about the following questions: What would our community be like if we had only football players in it? Where would we get our food?"

This exercise in brainstorming brought them closer to reality; they recognized that we need people in the community to get food to us. And someone in the class would usually remind us by yelling out, "Wow! We need somebody to do the farming, don't we?"

I would seize the moment by replying, "You get the picture! We need people with many skills in our community. And guess what? Each one of you has the potential of being a hero with whatever gifts God gives you."

The point is one does not have to be able to jump above the basketball rim and dunk a basketball, does not have to possess extraordinary physical prowess, does not have to possess extraordinary mental capacity, and does not have to become rich or famous in this world in order to be a hero. You can be hero with whatever gift or talent God gives to you.

We All Need Heroes to Help Meet Our Needs

We must first realize that we all need heroes in our lives; and we need to be heroes in other people's lives. We all need each other to meet each other's needs. We can begin to realize this only when we accept the fact that no person is an island unto oneself.

We are created to be relational beings, and therefore we relate to one another by helping meet each other's needs. This type of dynamic can take place only when each one of us allows our individual gifts to be used for each one's benefit, individually as well as collectively.

Why is it so difficult for this dynamic to take place in our society? We can begin to answer this question as we realize that for the most part, the Western society in which we live is primarily driven by the ideal of self-centeredness that focuses on me, myself, and I, which is described as individualism. As a result, society is telling us we can make it on our own. To overcome this mindset, we must learn we need others to help meet our needs.

It is Important That Each Individual Select His or Her Own Heroes

We must not allow the media to direct and drive our lives by setting the parameters and boundaries by which we select and recognize our heroes. We must select our own heroes.

It is my belief that by using the definition that we used earlier as a guideline in selecting our heroes, we will begin to understand more fully why someone is our true hero.

When we become able to define and recognize a hero in our midst, we will have the means by which to select our own heroes. Once we master this understanding, we can better recognize that each one of us must see and experience our individual heroes through our five natural senses and, yes, our spiritual sense. As a result you, as an individual will be able to determine your true heroes who have influenced you in a positive way.

Chapter 2

In the Midst of the Coronavirus Pandemic, Many Ask Who Is in Control

The arrival of the coronavirus pandemic on the scene has taught me, and I am sure many others, that although one can live here on earth a hundred-plus years, one still will not have seen it all. It has once again caused many to ask who is in control.

It is a reminder that things or events can and will happen in our lives that we never thought we would see. Events such as the coronavirus pandemic are reminders that we are not in control. Thus, one of the first lessons the coronavirus pandemic is teaching that we do not ultimately have control over what can happen in our lives. So the question we ask is, Who is in control?

Who Is in Control

The question that many often ask is, If man is not in control, then who is? It is this writer's belief that God, the greatest hero of all, is ultimately in control. Why? Because nothing can happen without God allowing it.

If God wills it to happen, it will happen. Does this mean that we must live our lives with a fatalistic approach? No. It means that although God gives humans free will, it has to operate within God's sovereign will.

O the depth of the riches both of the wisdom and knowledge of God! How unsearchable are His judgements, and His ways past finding out. (Romans 11:33 KJV)

For my thoughts are not your thoughts, nor your ways my ways says the Lord. For as the heavens are higher than the earth, so are my ways higher than yours, and my thoughts than your thoughts. (Isaiah 55:8–9 NASB)

With this in mind, before delving into how the coronavirus pandemic has impacted the whole world, take comfort in knowing that God is in control. Nothing can happen without God's permission. God is the Creator, He is sovereign, and He is the Ruler and Sustainer over all.

The earth is the LORD's and everything in it, the world and all who live in it. (Psalm 24:1 KJV)

No one can trick or force God to do anything. No one can stop God from doing anything; if He permits things to happen, it's because of His divine purpose for our ultimate good, even when we think He is not in charge He is.

When pandemics or other unexpected events occur, He is still in charge. When things seem to be falling apart in our life, He is still in charge.

He is able to bring good out of bad things. He can use all circumstances to fulfill His divine purpose.

> We know that all things work together for good
> to those who love God, to those who are called
> according to His purpose. (Romans 8:28 KJV)

Many in the midst of suffering often ask why God allows people to suffer, "especially good people." Here are some of the usual questions asked.

(1) If God is in control, why is He allowing this to happen?
(2) If God is a God of love, why doesn't He care?
(3) If God is all powerful, why doesn't He remove this suffering? (I will discuss in more detail about this in chapter 7.)

Next, let us look at how the coronavirus pandemic is affecting people and their lives worldwide to further underscore the importance of heroes in our lives.

Chapter 3

The Coronavirus Pandemic Appearance on the Scene Has Caused Dramatic Changes Worldwide

Many health experts and scientists have indicated the new strain of coronavirus disease as originating in bats or pangolins in Wuhan City, Hubei Province, China.

Retrospective investigation by Chinese authorities has identified human cases with onset of symptoms in early December 2019. While some of the earliest known cases had a link to a wholesale food market in Wuhan, some did not.[1]

The debate is still ongoing as to exactly how the coronavirus disease began to spread. Whatever the link the cases had, the first transmission to humans was in Wuhan, China. Since then, it has been ascertained that the virus has been mostly spreading through person-to-person contact. Within a few months, it spread worldwide.

And it has affected every aspect of our existence, either directly or indirectly.

For purpose of writing this book, it is important that I give a general timeline of the coronavirus pandemic events to help highlight the invaluable roles heroes (people) play in our society.

- January 11, 2020—China records its first death linked to COVID-19.
- January 21, 2020—Chinese scientists conform that the coronavirus can be transferred from person to person.
- January 30, 2020—The World Health Organization (WHO) declares a global public health emergency.
- January 31, 2020—US president Trump bans foreign nationals from entering the United States if they had been in China within the prior two weeks.
- February 2, 2020—The first coronavirus death outside China is recorded in the Philippines.
- February 6, 2020—A person in California dies from the coronavirus, becoming the first known American death.
- February 11, 2020—The WHO announces that the disease caused by the novel coronavirus will be called COVID-19.
- March 11, 2020—The WHO declares the coronavirus outbreak a pandemic.
- March 20, 2020—The United States recorded 19,285 cases of COVID-19 resulting in 249 deaths.
- April 2, 2020—The world passes 1 million COVID-19 infections.
- April 7, 2020—Roughly 95 percent of all Americans were under some form of lockdown as a result of state, county, or city orders.
- April 9, 2020—About 6.6 million Americans filed for unemployment claims in the past week, bringing the total number of employment claims filed in the past three weeks to over 17 million.
- April 10, 2020—The world's COVID-19 deaths surpassed 100,000.

- April 30, 2020—The number of COVID-19 deaths in the United States. were 60,966, with 1.04 million confirmed cases. The number of total tests completed was 6.25 million.
- May 21, 2020—The number of global COVID-19 cases surpassed 5 million.
- June 28, 2020—The number of global COVID-19 cases surpassed 10 million, and global deaths surpassed 500,000.
- July 27, 2020—Phase III clinical trials for the COVID-19 vaccine, developed by Moderna, began in the United States.
- August 10, 2020—Moderna and the Trump administration negotiated a deal to supply the United States with 100 million doses of its experimental COVID-19 vaccine.
- By August 12, 2020—More than 20.4 million cases were reported worldwide. More than 744,000 people had died. More than 12.6 million had recovered from C0VID-19.
- October 2, 2020—US president Donald Trump and First Lady Melania Trump tested positive for COVID-19.
- December 14, 2020—The United States grants its first emergency use authorization for a COVID-19 vaccine to the Pfizer-BioNTech candidate.
- December 18, 2020—The United States grants its second emergency use authorization for a COVID-19 vaccine to the Moderna candidate.
- By December 26, 2020—One out of every 1,000 Americans had died from COVID-19.

Global Status as of March 25, 2021

- Total cases confirmed globally: 125,234,087
- Total death confirmed worldwide: 2,749,397

Global Status as of April 22, 2021

- Total cases confirmed globally: 148 million
- Total deaths confirmed globally: 3.12 million[2]

Why Is It so Important to Show a General Timeline of the Coronavirus Pandemic Events?

In my view, it is critically important to show a general timeline of the coronavirus pandemic events to emphasize the far-reaching impact it is having on humankind. Further, it shows how a debilitating disease such as this is affecting every aspect of our existence.

Thus, by taking a cursory examination of the chronological timeline of reported coronavirus deaths, confirmed cases, and total COVID-19 tests, one can see the impact that COVID-19 is having worldwide. This far-reaching impact will be felt for years and generations to come, especially with the prospect of variants of the current COVID-19 possibly occurring into the future.

In addition, we must remember the chronology of events I have shown, which show that when people are affected in large numbers, it causes a ripple effect throughout our society, affecting every component of our lives, because people are our primary resource as well as the primary movers of other available resources on earth.

We are going to get a clearer picture of this dynamic as we look at our natural resources. However, before talking about our natural resources, it is important that we first exam what sets the coronavirus pandemic apart from prior pandemics, plagues, or disasters.

Chapter 4

What Sets the Coronavirus Pandemic Apart from Prior Pandemics, Plagues, or Disasters

To understand why the coronavirus pandemic stands out in a special way from prior pandemics, plagues, or other disasters, it is first important to understand what makes a pandemic different from plagues and other natural disasters. Let us examine the definition and a brief summary of each one.

> **Pandemic.** It is agreed by most scientists, in general, that a pandemic is when an infectious disease is spreading through human populations across large regions, or worldwide. The Center for Disease Control (CDC) defines a pandemic as "a disease outbreak that has spread across multiple countries and continents and usually impacts many people."[1]

How Does a Person Contract the Coronavirus Disease?

According to experts, the coronavirus is a respiratory virus. It spreads from person to person, and thus it enters through the respiratory tract.

There are several ways this can happen.

- **Droplets or aerosols**. This is the most common transmission. When an infected person coughs, sneezes, or talks, droplets, or tiny particles called aerosols, carry the virus into the air from their nose or mouth. Anyone who is within six feet of that person can breathe it into their lungs.

- **Airborne transmission**. Research shows that the virus can live in the air for up to three hours. It can get into your lungs if someone who has it breathes out, and you breathe in that air. Experts are divided on how much it contributes to the pandemic.

- **Surface transmission**. A less common method is when you touch surfaces that someone who has the virus has coughed or sneezed on. You may touch a countertop or doorknob that's contaminated and then touch your nose, mouth, or eyes. The virus can live on surfaces like plastics and stainless steel for two to three days. To stop it, clean and disinfect all counters, knobs, and other surfaces you or your family touch several times a day.

- **Fecal and oral**. Studies also suggest that virus particles can be found in infected people's poop. But experts aren't sure whether the infection can spread through contact with an infected person's stool. If that person uses the bathroom and doesn't wash their hands, they could affect things and people they touch.[2]

Once Inside the Body, How Does It Attack a Person?

Once inside the body, the virus begins infecting glandular cells. This first takes place in the upper respiratory tract, which includes the nose, mouth, larynx, and bronchi. As a result, the patient begins to experience mild version of symptoms: dry cough, shortness of breath, fever, headache, muscle pain, and tiredness, which is comparable to the flu.

Symptoms become more severe once the infection starts making its way to the lower respiratory tract, which includes the lungs. This condition can lead to pneumonia and autoimmune disease. Younger patients have a more vigorous immune response compared to older patients. Coupled with this, older patients most often have other underlined medical conditions, which in part explains why it affects the older population to a greater degree.

Let's compare a pandemic with a plague.

> **1. Plague.** We will start by defining *plague* as a noun.
>
> (1) An epidemic disease that causes high mortality, pestilence;
>
> (2) An infectious, epidemic, disease caused by a bacterium, *Yersina pestis*, characterized by fever, chills, and prostration, transmitted to humans from rats by means of the bites of fleas.
>
> (3) Any widespread affliction, calamity, or evil, especially one regarded as a direct punishment by God.[3]

When we use plague in this sense, it brings to mind biblical plagues, such as the plagues of Egypt, which were ten disasters God inflicted on Egypt, including swarms of locusts, hordes of frogs, a scourge of boils, pestilence of livestock, and the death of firstborn sons (see Exodus 7–11). One could write a volume of books on the biblical plagues alone. However, for purpose of this book, I will focus on comparing the pandemic with plagues and natural disasters in general.

To put this in the right perspective, the first question we must ask, What do the coronavirus and plagues have in common?

According to the editorial at *Dictionary.com* they both are infectious diseases that spread to humans from certain animals. However, COVID-19 is caused by a virus—essentially a tiny bit of nucleic acid and protein that needs a living host. In contrast, a plague is caused by bacteria, which are single-cell organisms. Moreover, while antibiotics work on bacteria, they do not work on viruses.[4]

The next question we need to ask is, What are the comparisons between the two? Like a plague, the coronavirus is an epidemic disease and more. However, what makes them different is that (1) a plague usually occurs in a smaller region or certain continents, and (2) it is called a *pandemic* when it spreads worldwide.

How does a pandemic compare with a natural disaster?

> **Natural Disaster.** According to Wikipedia, "a natural disaster is a major adverse event resultanting from natural processes of the Earth; such as floods, hurricanes, tornadoes, volcanic eruptions, earthquakes, tsumamis, storms, or some other geologic processes."[5]

According to the American Red Cross, they respond to more than sixty thousand disasters each year.

A natural disaster can cause loss of life, damage property, and even leave some economic damage in its wake. The severity depends on the affected area and population resiliency, such as having the infrastructure available for recovery. However, a natural disaster is usually confined to a smaller area than a plague or pandemic.

At the height of the coronavirus pandemic in 2020, several tornadoes swept through some southern US states, destroying neighborhoods, flattening homes, and killing dozens.

Also, in addition to dealing with the coronavirus pandemic, there was major flooding in some parts of China, displacing many from their homes, destroying homes and businesses, and in the process disrupting the normal lives of many.

To answer the question "How does the coronavirus pandemic differ from plagues and natural disasters?" we must compare the definitions of all three and summarized the effects of each one. When we do so, we will find that a pandemic affects people and their lives on a worldwide scale, either directly or indirectly.

With this in mind, I believe the coronavirus pandemic provides an ideal case study because it tells us much about heroes in our midst, both in America and worldwide.

Why the Coronavirus Pandemic Is an Ideal Case Study for Showing Us What It Tells Us about Heroes

What is a case study? "A case study is a detailed study of a specific subject, such as a person, group, place, event, organization, phenomenon."[6]

For the purpose of showing how the coronavirus pandemic presents an ideal case study in pointing to the many heroes in our midst, it is not my intent to delve into a large-scale research project. Rather, it is my intent to explore the key characteristics of this phenomenal event, that is, the coronavirus pandemic, to show how it is affecting our lives and will continue to do so for years to come. By doing so, without a doubt, we will further see the immeasurable roles that heroes from every walk of life play in our midst.

What Is the Coronavirus Pandemic Showing Us as We Look through the Lens of Our Physiological Needs and Our Other Needs?

I believe that rationally, we all can agree our physiological needs are the most basic and are vital to our survival: water, air, food, and sleep. Without the physiological needs being met people cannot survive for long. We must keep in mind the role that people play in meeting these needs. Therefore, humankind are not only the recipients of these needed resources but also must be the primary movers of these resources.

When I think about the important role that humankind plays as God's instrument in this world, I am reminded what He said to Moses at the burning bush concerning the suffering of the Hebrews in Egypt:

> The LORD said, I have surely seen the affliction of My people who are in Egypt and I have heard their cry on the account of their taskmasters, for I know their sorrows. Therefore, I have come down to deliver them out of the hand of the Egyptians, and bring them up out of that land to a good and spacious land, to a land flowing with milk and honey … *Come therefore and I will send you to Pharaoh so that you may bring forth My people, the children of Israel out of Egypt.* (Exodus 3:7–10 KJV; emphasis added)

It is a reminder that God most often comes to humans through humans. Humans are God's representatives on earth.

That is the very point I am making in showing how God is coming to us through the heroes from every walk of life in the midst of the coronavirus pandemic. Without people, the other resources on earth cannot be channeled to our needs.

Moreover, without people, our major systems and institutions on earth cannot function properly: economy, transportation, communication, political, education, religion, entertainment, health care, sports, and more.

Natural Resources

We have already seen that people are our main resource as well as the primary movers of other resources that others must have access to for their everyday physiological needs, in addition to other needs being met.

Again, remember that when we speak of physiological needs, we are referring to needs such as food, water, air, and sleep, which are fulfilled through our natural resources.

However, I am not unmindful that some reading this information might question this by saying sleep is not a natural resource. I invite you to listen to what God says in Psalm 127:2 (KJV), "He gives His beloved sleep."

Moreover, if we read about the Creation, particularly Genesis 1 and 2:1-7, we discover God is the source of all our natural resources. It all belongs to Him.

> The earth belongs to the Lord and everything therein. (Psalm 24:1 KJV)

However, the question that needs to be answered at this juncture is, How is the coronavirus pandemic affecting the flow of our access to natural resources? To understand how this is happening, let us first clarify what we mean when we use the words *natural resources*.

How Do We Define Natural Resources?

In my opinion, one of the best definitions of *natural resources* is found in the Toppr educational app for students:

> Natural resources are resources that exist without any actions of humankind. Air, water, food, plants, animals, minerals, metals, and everything else that exists in nature and has utility to mankind is a resource. The value of each such resource depends on its utility and other factors.[7]

There is much more to be said about natural resources and the classifications of them. However, in making my case about what the coronavirus pandemic tells us about heroes, I want to focus on the fact that natural resources are used to make food, fuels, and raw materials for the production of goods to meet our everyday needs.

Take food, for example. How often do we think about the many stages it passes through before it gets to our tables for our consumption? How often we take for granted that we need farmers (people) to grow the food, and to prepare it, before we can eat it?

Having grown up on a farm, I can vividly remember the sequential and cyclical stages and steps a farmer must progress through to grow produce such as fruits, vegetables, meats, and many other edible items to provide food for humankind, as well as food for the birds, the animals, and other living creatures.

1. The soil preparation
2. The sowing of seeds
3. Natural rain, or human-made irrigation systems using water
4. Fertilizing and cultivating plants

5. The harvesting of the produce or goods
6. Many other details regarding the art and science of farming

There are other types of farming such as raising pigs, cows, and chickens, and even wild animals, for meat produce. May we never forget that farming is a twenty-four seven, year-round job. From sunup to sunset, the farmer can be found in the fields and fruit orchards toiling all day, and even into the night, to get the job done in a timely basis. Rain or shine, the farmer's work is never ending and it takes constant vigilance.

And so may our hearts be filled with gratitude for farmers. Remember, it is due to their hard and dedicated laboring that we get food on our plates, the most important necessity for us to live and survive.

Surely we all can agree that without food, one of the main ingredients in our physiological needs, whether we are rich, poor, or somewhere in between, none of us cannot survive.

May we never forget to thank God, and thank the farmers from our heart.

Moreover, may we never forget farmers are among our greatest heroes, and the coronavirus pandemic is highlighting this very fact.

The coronavirus pandemic is, in a resounding way, reminding us how critical it is to keep our food supply flowing continuously.

How often do we recognize that it is the farmers and people who work in other food-related systems who make it possible for food and other goods to flow through an uninterrupted network of systems so we can have food to eat each day, as well the necessary goods for use in many other areas.

Moreover, may we never overlook the important fact that our food system and other systems are interconnected and must network with one another to meet our hierarchy of needs in a systematic way.

Most of all, may we never forget that each network in our various systems cannot operate properly when people cannot work. To underscore this very important point, we can get a clearer picture by taking a general look at several key statistics concerning the world population and the number of people who work on a job.

The World's Population and the Percentage of People Who Work on Some Type of Job

The estimated world population for 2020 is approximately 8 billion people.[8] The estimated US population is 331.5 million people.[9]

Now think about this: On a worldwide basis, it is estimated that approximately 70 percent of the population worldwide works on some type of job.[10]

It means that based on the world's population of 8 billion people in 2020, this gives a staggering figure of 5.6 billion people working on some type of job worldwide. This does not take into consideration that many are working more than one job. This also does not take into account those who do volunteer work, work off the books, or work on bartering terms.

As of March 31, 2020, more than one-third of humanity was under some form of lockdown (*Business Insider*, p. 38, 51). Some have said that the figure could go as high as 40 percent or more. Many could not go to work because of business closures or shutdowns due in part to the mandates of federal, state, or local officials.

Considering it is normally 5.6 billion people working on some type of job in the world, and one-third of 5.6 billion jobs were disrupted or shut down due the coronavirus pandemic, it means that as of March 31, 2020, about 1.86 billion people were not able to go to work each day. As the number of coronavirus cases rise, coupled with the increasing shutdowns of businesses, it is causing millions of people to file for unemployment.

Looking at America alone, according to The Pew Research Center, the "The COVID-19 outbreak and the economic downturn it engendered swelled the ranks of unemployed Americans by more than 14 million, from 6.2 million in February, 2020 to 20.5 million in May, 2020."[11]

This, in and of itself, gives us an astounding picture of how the coronavirus pandemic disrupted every component of our society and our lives in general. Further, it underscores the undeniable fact that if people cannot go to work, that has a direct effect on every aspect of our society.

Thus, because of the effect of the coronavirus pandemic labor markets in America and worldwide, the labor market was and still is being disrupted on a historically unprecedented scale.

Because we are becoming more globally connected worldwide than ever before, and because we are increasingly becoming more dependent on the modern, computerized, digitized systems controlling nearly every aspect of our lives, any rupture in its networking system can cause a reverberating effect on the full spectrum of our existence. Look at a general sketch of how the coronavirus pandemic is affecting the operation of every primary system in our society and consequently our lives.

The Coronavirus Pandemic Is Affecting the Operation of Every Primary System and Subsystem in Our Society and, as a Result, Affecting Our Lives.

It is affecting every area in our society: economy, commerce, education, health care, communication, transportation, government, religion, entertainment, sports, and more.

- The flow of food supplies, tools, material goods, and manufacturing goods has been disrupted in both the essential and nonessential categories.

- Nonessential businesses were ordered to close. And this included restaurants and other private food outlets.
- Essential classified businesses were limited in its capacity to serve its goods or products. Restaurants and fast food chains indoor services were closed. Each one had to transition to drive-through or home delivery services.
- Schools were ordered to remain closed for many months, resorting in thousands of young people having to stay home and transition to online schooling to variant extents, depending on the state or county mandate issued by its leadership's whims.
- Health-care services and hospitals were forced to limit their services mainly to emergency care only. According to experts in the medical administrative area, the coronavirus pandemic has created historical financial pressure for our hospitals and health-care system. Hospitals have cancelled nonemergency procedures, and many Americans postponed care as they sheltered in place to stop the spread of the virus.Treatment of covid-19 patients has created a demand for specialized medical equipment. It has affected the supply chain, resulting in cost increase for hospitals. Additionally, because of job losses, it has caused many to be uninsured.
- Government agencies were partially shut down and began operating on a limited basis.
- The military, in some areas, were required to operate in a paramilitary mode.
- Sports arenas were closed, and others sports activities were restricted.
- The airline industry was grounded or restricted to limited use.
- The land transportation system in general was disrupted and thereby forced to use improvised means for delivering its cargo and goods.

- The shipping industry's mode and speed of shipping were forced to use alternative methods of shipping.
- Theaters and other entertainment outlets closed, forcing the entertainment industry to use new ways to channel its movies through the Internet, home computers, and other improvised media-disseminating methods.
- Tourism and hospitality companies were brought almost to a standstill.
- Churches and organized religious indoor activities were limited or forced to shut down in some states, causing many to used alternative means of conducting worship service.

Folks, this is serious stuff!

In addition, the disruption in how we shop has forever changed the dynamics of traditional shopping. More and more of our meals are being ordered online with options to use home delivery service, drive-through pickup service, or curbside pickup service.

Certainly, all this and more has disrupted how our hierarchy of needs are met: physiological, security, social, self-esteem, self-actualization, and spiritual self-actualization.

Like a thief in the night, COVID-19 came when we were not prepared for it, nor were we expecting it. It is a wake-up call, reminding us we cannot always control circumstances invading our lives. More than any other modern event, the coronavirus pandemic is reminding us of the importance of being better prepared for future pandemics.

Chapter 5

Ways We Are Responding

Although I am primarily speaking of how we responded and are still responding in America, I believe my observation rings true worldwide. Why is this true? No matter where people live, they have an innate tendency to come together in times of tragedy or special emergency. This is good news in that the same response is prevailing in the midst of the coronavirus pandemic. Heroes from every walk of life are showing up and serving in heroic ways.

People from Every Walk of Life Are Showing up and Serving in Heroic Ways

Let me refresh your memory of how a hero is defined, as spelled out earlier by The Shorter Dictionary: "A hero is a person recognized or admired for his or her courage, ability, or achievements and noble qualities in any field."

And here is how I define a hero from a simple, real-life prospective: A hero is someone who says something to you, or does something for you or to you, that helps or encourages you to go forward in life in a positive way.

Now that we have a firmer grasp of how to define a hero, it should give us a trustworthy set of guidelines to help us recognize a hero when we see one.

As I journey through life, there are three common traits I have found in each true hero: (1) Each one is willing to help other people; (2) each one is willing to use his or her individual, God-given ability or gift for the common good of everyone; and (3) each one recognizes that he or she serves a cause greater than oneself.

People from All Walks of Life Are Responding amid the Coronavirus Pandemic

When we talk about how people are responding to defeat the coronavirus, invariably we must take into consideration our leaders as well as people from every walk of life.

In my opinion, the best way to begin looking at the many ways people are responding to the coronavirus pandemic is to first know that everyone is involved on some level. Why is this so? Fighting the coronavirus pandemic is like fighting in a war. The difference in this war is it is nonvoluntary. We all are drafted into this war, from ages one to one hundred. No one is exempt. How each one of us responds will determine what types of soldiers we are.

There are many ways people are responding. The leader of our country sets the tone. Our leader at the outset of the coronavirus pandemic was Donald Trump. Clearly, as the leader of America, he has the executive power and authority to make decisions that can have the most impact on how America moves forward to eradicate the coronavirus.

I could talk about President Trump's decision to issue a travel ban from China as soon as that country was identified as being ground zero for the coronavirus. I could talk about him issuing further travel restrictions from other global hotspots, including the European Union, Ireland, and Iran. Or I could talk about more than seventy-five other decisions he made.

However, I believe the most impactful decision he made to help eradicate the coronavirus, and thereby save lives, is when he formally announced Operation Warp Speed on May 15, 2020, in the White House Rose Garden. President Trump described the administration plan "as a massive scientific industrial and logistical endeavor unlike anything our country has seen since the Manhattan Project of World War II, with the intent to rapidly develop and distribute a vaccine with help from the US military and world-renowned doctors and scientists."[1]

His authority and unique leadership ability made him the right man for this time to enlist and rally the public and private sectors of America—doctors and scientists, military leaders, pharmaceutical companies, and others—to focus on a common mission: to rapidly develop a vaccine to help eradicate the coronavirus by the end of 2020.

What is Operation Warp Speed (OWS)? It is a federal and private sector program initiated to facilitate and accelerate the testing, supply, development, and the distribution of safe and affective vaccines, therapeutics, and diagnostic tools to begin eradicating the coronavirus by January 2021.[2] The name was inspired by terminology for faster-than-light used in the Star Trek fictional universe, evoking a sense of rapid progress.[3]

There were many who doubted a vaccine could be developed by January 2021, largely because historically it had taken two years or more to develop a vaccine of this nature. Nonetheless, a three-pronged miracle happened.

- December 11, 2020—The US Food and Drug Administration issued an emergency us authorization in the United States for the first vaccine, Pfizer.
- December 18, 2020—The US Food and Drug Administration issued an emergency use authorization in the United States for the second vaccine, Moderna.

- February 27, 2021—The U.S. Food and Drug Administration issued an emergency use authorization in the United States for the third vaccine, Johnson and Johnson/Jansen.[4]

It is my opinion that this historical achievement will go down as one of the greatest in America. This momentous act has saved millions of lives.

Thanks and honor are due to the heroes who made this possible: President Trump, our many government agents, our doctors and scientists, our clinical trials volunteers, and all who worked diligently to make this happen. Thanks for your heroic acts. Because of your personal compassion to help and your many hours of sacrifice, many lives were saved. And there are many others who participated in this tremendous achievement who also responded in heroic ways. Thank you for your heroic acts.

Chapter 6

Observing and Dialoguing with Heroes in Our Midst

Once again, I am reminded how often we take for granted the invaluable service and heroic acts of those who often go unrecognized. Some of the most rewarding moments amid the coronavirus pandemic are those I have experienced by observing and dialoguing with heroes from different walks of life as they serve in their various jobs.

From the outset, as you journey with me, I remind you that I am a minister of the Gospel, and therefore I observe and dialogue from both the physical and spiritual perspectives.

It has been said that our true character shows up in extreme times of testing in our life; it can bring out the best in us, or it can bring out the worst in us. With a few exceptions, most of those I observed and dialogued with demonstrated a positive character.

Remember, the coronavirus pandemic came like a thief in the night. We were not expecting it, nor were we prepared for it.

Yet it is amazing how we are rallying together in the midst of the pandemic. So journey with me as I observe and dialogue with the many heroes who are showing up and helping each other by using their God-given gifts and talents.

Things began to take a bad turn as we got the news in the

first part of March 2020 that the coronavirus was beginning to spread throughout America.

By mid-March, businesses, schools, churches, sports arenas, and other areas were shutting down. Hospitals were limiting their service to emergency needs only. People everywhere began to panic shop. Store shelves were rapidly becoming empty and not being restocked.

Labor experts were estimating that by the end of March 2020, nearly one-third of the population in America was under the order of a lockdown. This is when my observation and dialoging became more focused. I noticed that even with the lockdown orders, many workers were required to go on the "front lines" and work in their respective jobs so our basic needs, as well as other needs and desires, could be met.

Observing and Dialoguing with a Truck Driver

As I entered a side parking lot of a grocery store in my neighborhood, I had the pleasure of observing and dialoguing with a truck driver who was waiting for food and other goods to be unloaded from his truck. Oh, how often we take for granted the truckers who drive night and day to deliver food and others goods to us so people can have food to eat and other items of necessities in life.

I made a concerted effort to enter a dialogue with the truck driver. As I approached him, I noticed he was probably nearing his fiftieth birthday. Upon approaching him, I said, "Good morning, sir. Thank you for your service."

He replied, "Good morning to you, sir. I appreciate you thanking me, but I never served in the military." I responded by reminding him that he indeed was performing a great ministry. He chuckled as he smiled and said, "I am not a minister either, but I appreciate you giving me credit for what I do."

"Yes," I said, "I want you to know that our greatest ministry is on the outside of the walls of a church. So keep on using your gift as a truck driver to serve others. Remember: God does not just reward us for how much we do. He also rewards us for how faithful we are in what we do. So keep up the good work, and thanks for your service. And tell all your fellow truck drivers that we thank them for their service as they deliver food and goods to meet our everyday needs."

He had a smile of satisfaction on his face as he walked back to his truck. He said, "Wow! I never thought I was that important."

I quickly seized the moment by saying, "Your job has always been important, although some people take your job for granted. You have heard the old saying: 'We don't miss the water until the well goes dry.'"

The truck driver chuckled as he said, "One thing is for sure: the coronavirus has caused the flow of food items coming to distribution centers to trickle in at a slower pace because of bottlenecking in the supply chain. Remember, this is where I get my loads of foods and other goods from. This means I now have to work longer hours because I have to travel with smaller loads and make more trips in order to get the food items and other goods to each store. For me, it's a sense of urgency because people gotta eat in order to live.

"Think about it: Other truck drivers who haul other materials and goods are facing the same challenges as me. But there is one thing I know about truckers: we are a bunch of tough and dedicated dudes, and we will do all we can to get our goods to its destination."

After hearing the truck driver remind me of the urgency at hand and his willingness to meet the challenge, my dialogue with him took on a more solemn tone. I said, "I want you know I appreciate the great work you are doing. And remember, God knows the great work you are doing; and may God bless you in all that you do. Be safe."

As he climbed behind the steering wheel in his truck, he said with an encouraged look on his face, "Thanks. I needed that, and may God bless you too. Be safe."

As I entered the store, I noticed one of the stock persons driving a loaded forklift with food and other items to be stocked in the store.

Observing and Dialoging with a Stockperson

The man who was unloading the truck was using his forklift to carry his last load into the storage area. I said to myself, *I wonder if he knows how important his job is.*

It began thundering in the sky as the rain began falling. As I approached the forklift driver, I noticed that he had what appeared to be a stressed look on his face. A little voice within me said, "Why don't you say something to him to cheer him up?"

The first thing that came to my mind was to say, "How are you doing this beautiful day?"

He turned and looked at me with a puzzled look on his face as he replied, "What's so beautiful about it? Don't you see its beginning to rain, and the sun is not shining?"

I said, "Yes, that's true, but remember the sun is still shining. You just can't see it."

He responded, "Nice try, mister, but right now nothing seems to be shining in my life. It seems like the harder I work on this job, the less I am appreciated."

"How so?" I asked.

"Well, for one thing, with this coronavirus pandemic going on, I have to work long hours as a forklift driver, unloading the food from the trucks coming in here on an irregular basis. To add to that, I have to double up as a stockperson inside the store. Sometimes I think this is an unthankful job, especially when shoppers come into the store and harass us because the shelves are partially empty. They don't seem to appreciate us for doing our best to keep the shelves stocked."

It was clear by now that this stockperson needed to be encouraged and shown some appreciation. As I made an extra effort to put a solemn look on my face, I said to him, "Can I tell you something?"

"Yeah, what?" he replied.

"I want to say thanks to you for what you do."

"Are you serious?" he said. "Nobody seems to think my job is important. In fact, there are some around here who think I am not important."

I interjected by saying, "I think you are important, and I think you have one of the most important jobs there is."

He chuckled. "You are trying to play with my mind. Nice try, mister."

At this juncture, I knew I needed to again seize the moment to remind him why I think his job is important. "Can I tell you something, brother? Think about it: Without the job you are doing, many people would not have food to eat. So don't let anyone put you down, because in reality, if we do not have people like you, many would not have food to buy and prepare for their meals. So yes, your job is very important. I encourage you to always remember that the work you do makes it possible for people to survive. Without food to eat, no one can live for long. And remember: Although others may not recognize the importance of your work, I see you as a hero."

With a surprised look on his face, he replied, "I never thought I would ever hear anyone call me a hero. Why do you think I am a hero?"

I responded, "A hero is someone who helps others meet their needs. And so you are a hero."

He replied, "I never looked at it that way. Thanks for giving my job a new meaning."

"Also remember that God sees the good work you are doing, and surely He will bless you."

With a calm look of satisfaction on his face, as he continued stocking the shelves, he said, "Thanks for reminding me that my job is important. You are breath of fresh air. I hope you find the food items you are looking for. If you need help in finding anything, check with me, and I will see if I can locate it for you."

"Thanks for the offer," I replied.

Fortunately, I was able to find the few items I needed. Now, my next challenge was to get through the checkout line.

Observing and Dialoguing with a Young Cashier

As I headed toward the checkout line, from a distance I could see that the lines were filled to capacity with restless and impatient-looking shoppers.

A thought came to me: "It is not an absolute necessity that I need to buy these items today, so why don't you take these items and put them back on the shelves? Or better yet, leave them in the shopping cart right where you are and walk out, thereby avoid having to wait in a long line in order to be processed by a cashier."

Then a little, smart-sounding voice within said, "I suggest you get in line like everybody else is doing and wait your turn. Also, remember that a few days from now, you might not be able to find the items you are tempted to leave behind. Think about it: the shelves in the store are getting more empty by the minute."

The smart voice within won out. I went to the end of one of the lines and waited my turn.

As I waited in line, I noticed that the young cashier serving the line was a student I had formerly tutored in math.

I am aware the retail and grocery stores often hire young high school students on a part-time basis as cashiers. I did some quick math in my head, remembering the year I had tutored her in math; at that time, she had been in the eighth grade. I concluded that she was now in the eleventh grade and therefore about seventeen years old. I quickly noticed that she was being challenged by some of the shoppers in the line as they impatiently waited for her to process their groceries.

Some of the shoppers were rude and disrespectful toward the young cashier, unfairly blaming her for the shortages in the store and what they thought were misplaced price tags. By observing the countenance on her face, I could tell these unfair verbal attacks on her were taking their toll with each passing moment. It was clear I needed to calm her down with encouraging words rather than bombard her with accusatory words, as some of the shoppers in line were doing.

After a long wait, it was my term to place my food items and other household items on the conveyor belt. The young cashier recognized me. "Hi, Pastor Charles. It is so good to see you again. You may not remember it, but you tutored me in math when I was in the eighth grade. Thanks. Because of your help, I am passing all my math classes, and now I am a junior in high school and am looking forward to graduating next year."

"I recognize your face, but I have forgotten your name," I said with an apologetic smile.

She quickly replied, "My name is Shirley Pawson. Remember?"

"Thanks for refreshing my memory." Knowing that the line was long, I did not want to prevent her from serving the other shoppers, especially because some of them had already verbally abused her. After paying my bill, I quickly reached into my card folder, handed her one of my business cards, and said, "Please give my regards to your parents for me, and encourage them to call me at their convenience. It will be good hearing from them. Also, this will give me an opportunity to talk to you after you get off work."

Before leaving the line, I knew that I needed to quickly say something to encourage Shirley and let the other shoppers know that they too should be grateful for the job she was doing as a cashier. I looked at Shirley with a grateful smile and said with a loud but assuring voice, "Thank you for the work you are doing. Keep up the good work. You are a hero."

"Thanks for your encouragement," she said.

I quickly exited the store. However, I knew that I needed to say more to Shirley to let her know how important her cashier's job was to people.

Several days passed. It was late evening. As I was relaxing at home, the thought would not let me go. I continued to ponder on the need to encourage Shirley and remind her how important her job as a cashier is, and at the same time remind her it can be used as an entry-level job to bigger things to come.

Suddenly, my phone rang. I looked at my caller ID and noticed it appeared to be from the Pawson residence. I immediately picked it up and said, "Hello, this is Pastor Charles. Whom am I speaking to?"

"I am Jason Pawson, Shirley's father," replied the voice on the other end.

"I am so pleased you called, and I do hope you, Mrs. Pawson, and the rest of the family are doing okay."

"Yes, we are doing very well, and I hope you and your family are doing well. Before I forget, Pastor Charles, I want to say thanks for the math tutoring my daughter received from you a few years ago. Please accept my apology for not saying this to you before now."

"You are quite welcome. Shirley was a good student, and I was pleased to hear that she has been successful in her math classes. She and many other students do well when they are prepared with a good foundation in basic math."

As I reflect on my past teaching experience and now as a retired school teacher, my main purpose in helping Shirley, and other students I tutor in math is to give them a good foundation. According to the feedback I get from most of my former students, they say it was the foundation I gave them in basic math that helped them to be successful in it afterward.

Mr. Pawson said, "One thing is for sure: our daughter, Shirley, often reminds us of how thankful she is to you for tutoring her in math."

"Thank you, Mr. Pawson, for that reminder. Again, I am so glad that you called me, because I am so proud of how Shirley handled herself as she was working in the grocery store where I was shopping. I could not help but notice how rude some of the shoppers were to her. Yet she stayed calm and conducted herself well. As I left the store, I knew that it would be good to talk to her and encourage her to continue doing a good job, and it will pay off one day in many ways."

"She is sitting near me now with a smile on her face as we talk," said her father. "Do you mind if I step aside and allow her to talk to you?"

Without hesitation, I said, "Sure, it will be a pleasure."

Shirley said, "Hello, Pastor Charles. I am so glad my father called. I told him and my mother I saw you in the store."

In reply, I said, "Hello, Shirley. I am so glad they called, because I wanted to say more to you in the store, but I was very much aware that you were doing a good job as a cashier, and I did not want to interfere with your work in any way."

Piggy backing on my statement, Shirley seized the moment to express her intention. "I am so excited to be able to talk to you away from the demanding shoppers in the store. As you perhaps noticed, some of them can be rude and demanding. In fact, I told my dad and mom that I wanted to look for another job."

After hearing her say that, I knew it was important for me to encourage her and remind her how important her job is. No matter how challenging it can become, we must never let the challenge override the importance of our job.

"Shirley, as I think of the many jobs I had in the past, especially when I was young, my memory takes me back when I thought about quitting several times because I felt that my boss and some of the people I had to deal with on a daily basis were not respecting me. And for the many years I worked as a public school teacher, before retiring, there were times when I felt like my students, or my principal, or a supervisor, or the parents did not appreciate the work that I was doing to help our young people prepare for the future."

She said with affirmation, "Pastor Charles, I have personally seen what teachers have to put up with on a daily basis in their line of teaching." With an honest confession, she added, "I don't think I would have the patient to teach. Y'all teachers have to put up with a whole lotta stuff. However, there is one thing I do know: Without the many good teachers I have had over the years—and yes, your tutoring—I would not have made it this far. So I want to say thanks to you and all my faithful teachers. And by the way, teachers like you and others are heroes indeed."

"Thank you for your compliment. However, I must say something else to you with which I hope to encourage you. Over the years, I have learned when you are working with the public as I have as a teacher, and pastor, or in other lines of work, what kept me on even keel was knowing that the work I was doing was helping others live a better life. It is not easy dealing with the public because you meet people with so many different personalities. Some can rub you the wrong way. What really encouraged me to hang in there when the going got tough is I would tell myself, The work I am doing is a ministry. I am not working for myself or man. I am working for God."

Upon hearing that statement, Shirley took a deep breath and replied, "Wow! I have never thought about a job that way." After a slight pause, she added, "I am going to record that thought in my memory bank."

"Finally, Shirley, I want you to remember the job you have as a cashier is ever so important. You are making it possible for people—the good ones and the bad ones—to get food on their tables to eat. So I encourage you to hang in there. And remember that life is a step ladder. The job you have can be used as a step to greater things ahead. I encourage you to do what you can until you can do what you want. I wish you well on your job, and I will be so happy if you will let me know when you graduate from high school next year. I am so happy that I got a chance to talk with you. May God bless you in all your future endeavors. And always remember: You are a hero."

"Pastor Charles, I thank you for encouraging me. And may you never forget that you are a hero indeed. By the way, with your encouragement, I intend to continue working in this cashier job until I graduate from high school." Then she politely asked, "Would you like to speak to my father or mother again?"

"Yes, it will be a pleasure," I said.

Observing and Dialoguing with Parents and Grandparents

After a short pause, a female voice answered the phone. "Hello, this is Shirley's mother speaking."

"Hello, Mrs. Pawson. After hearing me talk to Mr. Pawson and your daughter, I am sure by now you know this is Pastor Charles."

"Yes," she quickly replied. "I'd recognize your voice anywhere. And I could hear the conversation you had with my husband and with my daughter, because they had the speaker phone on. I was taking in all you shared with my husband and my daughter."

In a humbling tone, I replied, "I hope I was not too long-winded in speaking to them, Mrs. Pawson."

"Oh, no, it was a pleasure listening. And may I say, I am sure your input encouraged Shirley to understand how important her cashier job is in helping people meet their basic needs. By the way, I can never thank you enough for tutoring Shirley when she was in the eighth grade."

"I appreciate your gratitude," I replied, "and may I remind you that I want to thank you for the many hours when you personally brought your daughter to her tutoring class. It is a reminder that when parents go that extra mile in helping their children get extra help in schooling, it will help them make better grades in school.

"Also, I am aware of the challenge parents are having in helping their children get proper schooling as a result of the coronavirus pandemic. Your schools, like many others, have been closed for several months, making it necessary for our youth to stay home and use alternative methods of learning such as online schooling and home teaching. I know it is not easy for you and other parents who have children in school. I want to encourage you and Mr. Pawson for the heroic job that you are doing as parents."

"Thank you for the encouragement," said Mrs. Pawson.

"With your permission, I would like for Mr. Pawson to be in on this conversation to further commend you and him together for the wonderful job you two are doing as parents."

"Sure," said Mrs. Pawson. I could hear her saying with a loud voice to Mr. Pawson, "Honey, pick up the other phone. Pastor Charles wants you to be in on the rest of this conversation."

After a brief pause, I could hear Mr. Pawson say, "I am on the second phone. Please continue, Pastor Charles. I am so grateful that you are taking time to talk to us."

"I consider it an honor and a pleasure. I briefly want to share my opinion with you both as to the immeasurable role that you, as parents, are playing in our society. The coronavirus pandemic has highlighted this very fact. Look at what is happening in our midst; and how it has impacted families everywhere. As a result, schools and parents have been forced to look for alternative ways for young people to receive an education. And coupled with this, parents have to work away from home every day, especially those who do not have the option of working from within their home. This has added to the challenge that parents are facing. In addition, there are some who have been laid off from their jobs, and therefore they are forced to seek unemployment benefits to make ends meet."

Mr. Pawson said, "You are so right. Mrs. Pawson and I are fortunate in that we can shuffle our working hours to make it possible that at least one adult is home to supervise the children and help monitor their online learning, as well as their other necessary activities. We are also playing the dual role of parents and grandparents. For example, we are keeping one of our daughter's children, who is in the first grade, while our daughter works during the day."

Mrs. Pawson added, "That is so true, and my husband forgot to mention that we also keep one of our neighbor's children, who is a second grader. Although this has challenged us greatly, we felt led to do this because our neighbor is a single parent, and needless to say, she is caught in between a rock and a hard place: quit her job so she can be home with her second grade child, or try to get someone to keep her child while she works."

Mr. Pawson interjected. "We are glad that we are able to help assist her by keeping her daughter, as well as our daughter's child. In times like these, each one must help each other."

"I am so pleased to hear that you and Mrs. Pawson are going the extra mile to help out. How often we forget that no matter what happens in our midst, whether the coronavirus pandemic or any other event, the parents still need to make sure their children's ongoing educational needs are met, even outside of school." I listed three specific aspects.

1. Making sure their children are properly supervised by an able adult.
2. Making sure their children are exposed to a healthy learning environment at home or some other place.
3. Making it possible for their children to have the opportunity to participate in supervised activities and to socialize with other children of their peer group whenever possible.

Mrs. Pawson replied solemnly, "It is really true. It takes a whole village to raise a child."

Mr. Pawson followed up by saying, "Amen to that."

"Yes, you are so right," I said. "And with that in mind this too should help us appreciate the role of parents, grandparents, other family members, and friends who help each other meet their needs in the community. Unfortunately, the important role that parents, grandparents, other family members, and neighbors play in our society is often not given its due credit. May we take time out and say thanks to them, because they are among our real heroes.

"Increasingly, we are living in a time when the importance of family is not fully recognized or appreciated. In my opinion, it is because many have failed to recognize that God created the family to be the basic unit in our society. Family is the glue that holds our society together. So goes our family, so goes our nation; so goes our family, so goes our community; so goes our family, so goes our churches; so goes our family, so goes our nation. It is clear that you, other parents, and those who are playing the role of parenthood are involved in one of the most important ministries in our society."

"Thank you, Pastor Charles, for your words of wisdom and encouragement," replied Mrs. Pawson.

"Yes," Mr. Pawson concurred. "And thank you for your ministry of teaching and proclaiming the Word of God, and for helping us to be the very best parents and grandparents we can be. For this, we will forever be grateful."

"I thank you. May I end by saying I encourage you to continue to stay close to God. And remember: You can do all things through Christ Jesus, who strengthens you (Philippians 4:13). Again, I thank you. It certainly was an honor and pleasure to talk with you all. Please do not hesitate to call me anytime."

"Likewise, and we look forward to hearing from you again. Good bye for now," said the Pawsons.

The Importance of Observing and Dialoging with Youth

Many in our society have characterized our youth of today as self-centered, having an attitude of entitlement, having an attitude of ingratitude, being lazy, having no sense of purpose in life, having no sense of responsibility or accountability, being anti-religious, having no respect for the value of life, and other negative connotations.

On the surface, one could say some of these observations are true. However, we should take time to understand that for the most part, the ethos in our society has played a major role in how our young people think and live today. As a society, we have failed to instill in our youth the importance of religious values, family values, dignity of work, politics, education, a sense of individual responsibility, rule of law, and a sense of patriotism devoted to the well-being and interest of one's country.

I think if we take time out from our hectic and busy schedules, our "get it done right now" way of life, and spend more time with young people, we will discover that they are searching for answers to help make this world a better place in which to live. If we dialogue with them on a regular basis, we will be able to guide them in wisdom and truth and help instill in them a sense of hope and purpose.

We can accomplish this by letting them see us as examples toward that end. It has been said humankind is an imitative being; from the cradle to the grave, one is learning to do what one sees or hears others do. In short, for the most part, our youth want to follow our lead.

When we adults set positive examples for our youth, we can help prepare them to carry the banner of hope in God, family, and country. We must remind each other that together with God, we can make this world a better place in which to live.

Please remember I am not speaking these words just to please or placate you. I have reason to believe I am speaking with authoritativeness, both in the spiritual and natural realms.

How so? I am speaking from the perspective and experience of having served as a minister of gospel for over forty years, and from having served as a pastor of several local churches much of this time. In addition, I have served as a public and private school teacher for thirty years, and I still teach today on a voluntary basis. By the way, I have had the honor, duty, and privilege of raising five children, and now I am helping to raise nine grandchildren.

Having said that, I believe I have much credibility when I say our young people can be counted on to make this world a better place in which to live, if we do our part as adults. The current coronavirus pandemic is serving as an impetus in emboldening my belief in our youth as I observe and dialogue with them during these challenging days.

An Inside Look with Me as I Observe and Dialogue with Youth

As a pastor at large, as a retired school teacher, and as a parent and grandparent, how can I but love working with young people, especially when I know they are our future? Therefore, my interest in seeing them do well in life naturally thrusts me into the midst of their everyday activities, albeit some of these activities I prearrange. Other activities come my way in terms of where the need arises.

By now, we all know that as a result of our schools, churches, and other organized indoor and outdoor youth activities closing down, it has thrust family life into a state of emergency, resulting in our youth being confined in their homes with limited mobility, as well as limited outdoor activities.

Nonetheless, I give kudos to our youth based on what I see and experience as I observe them, dialogue with them, and discover how well they are handling the coronavirus pandemic's challenges. Travel with me as I encounter several young people in the midst of the coronavirus pandemic.

Observing and Dialoguing with Several Young Children as They Grocery Shop with Their Mother in a Local Grocery Store

I hurriedly began shopping for a few grocery items needed to prepare my next meals at home, making sure to wear my mask and attempting to adhere to the safe distance rules. I was encouraged by what I saw.

As I was nearing the aisle that had an assortment of candy goods, I noticed a young mother with three young children, one boy and two girls, attempting to do their shopping. In using my years of experience of teaching youth, and as a parent, I estimated the youngest girl to be five years old, the young boy to be seven years old, and the oldest girl to be nine years old.

By now it was obvious the two younger ones had persuaded their young mother to take a detour through the candy aisle. It also became clear to me that the seven-year-old boy's craving for the sweet taste of candy goods on the self was becoming stronger, so much so that he was beginning to struggle with saliva in his mouth. As a result, he removed the mask from his face.

Suddenly, his five-year-old sister yelled out, "Boy, you better put your mask back on!"

The seven-year-old brother was startled and began stammering. He responded, "Oops." He looked around to see who else was watching him. As if to defend himself, he said, "I washed my hands as we came into the store."

By now, his mother became aware of what had happened, and she replied, "Yes, you did, but you know you are to wear your mask inside the store."

As the seven-year-old boy put his mask on again, he noticed I was looking on.

I said to his five-year-old sister, "You are a hero."

She replied, "Thanks, mister. I never thought I could be a hero."

I looked at each one of them and said, "You all are being heroes by wearing your mask. Think about it: By wearing your mask, you are helping to protect yourself, and you are also helping to protect others."

By now we had caught the attention of other shoppers, and they were impressed by what they had heard and seen. To avoid any further commotion, I waved to the young family with a smile of satisfaction and said, "Be safe."

As I departed from the store, I was once again reminded that we all, both young and old, can be heroes in some form by using our abilities to help and encourage each other along the way.

Seeing the Need to Help Provide Outdoor Activities for Youth during the Coronavirus Pandemic

One of the tragic results occurring during the coronavirus pandemic is not just the debilitating illnesses and deaths but also how it has limited our youth's ability to have access to outdoor sports activities or outdoor activities in general.

We often forget that our young people have growing and developing minds and bodies. They need space and time to provide them the opportunity to be exposed to outdoor activities—activities that will allow them to rip and run, laugh and yell, or just play crazy little games that only kids can think of.

In addition, we need to give them the opportunity to participate in supervised gardening or walking in the woods, seeing how many trees, plants, and flowers they can identify.

Youths need exposure to activities such as these to help

develop their growing bodies and minds and become more aware of the beauty of God's creation all around them.

As a retired public school teacher, a pastor, a parent of five children, and a grandparent of nine grandchildren, over the years I have had upfront experiences of observing and dialoguing with youth at every stage of their lives.

I have sat where they are sitting; I have walked where they are walking. Not only that, but I have seen what they do. I have heard them express their feelings. I have heard them talk about their dreams. I have seen them searching for meaning and purpose in life. Moreover, I have seen them struggle to cross the bridges of life from the cradle to adolescents, to preteens, to teens, and to adulthood.

As a teacher, I was keenly aware that the general purpose of the school is to provide the opportunity for our youth to be exposed to activities and curricula that help develop the total person, mind, body, and soul.

Stop and think of what is happening. The coronavirus pandemic suddenly invaded every area of our society, either directly or indirectly. But let us not forget how it has affected our youth. It has caused many of our schools, churches, and other youth-related agencies to close, resulting in our youth being restricted to their homes or other confined facilities.

As a result, our youth no longer have access to activities that will help them to develop the total person in mind, body, and soul.

And sadly, many adults have been so burdened with trying to survive the shutdown mandates, and other residual challenges until it has caused them to have less time to focus on helping the youth meet their special needs. In fact, many adults I talk to about the needs of our youth usually say, "There are too many of them who need help," or, "What can I do?"

In responding to this sense of hopelessness, I remind them about a story originally told by Loren Elsley regarding the starfish that a youth was throwing back in the ocean. The following is one of the story's many adaptations.

> One day a man was walking along the beach when he noticed a boy picking something up and gently throwing it into the ocean.
>
> Approaching the boy, he asked, "What are you doing?"
>
> The youth replied, "Throwing starfish back into the ocean. The surf is up and the tide is going out. If I don't throw them back, they'll die."
>
> "Son," the man said, "don't you realize there are miles and miles of beach and hundreds of starfish? You can't make a difference!"
>
> After listening politely, the boy bent down, picked up another starfish, and threw it back into the surf.
>
> Then, smiling at the man, he said ... "I made a difference for that one."[1]

The boy in this story did not know it, but he was doing what real heroes do: lend a helping hand with whatever ability we have in times of need.

I often tell the starfish story whenever adults in the community say there are too many youth to help.

I am happy to announce that there are some men and women with me in our community who are stepping up to the plate and providing a few of our youth with the opportunity to participate in outdoor activities. In our community, we are more fortunate than many. We have more open space. Some of us are blessed with the ownership of many acres of land.

We are giving youth the opportunity to learn how to do gardening, plant trees, grow and cultivate flowers and vegetables, and do other farm tasks. I believe giving our youth the opportunity to build and grow things is not only therapeutic but also gives them a sense of ownership and a sense of purpose in life.

Think about it: the coronavirus pandemic has caused youth—and everyone, for that matter—to stay inside more, and thereby they are exposed to video games, movies, and many other media outlets that bombard us with action and depict images of destruction and tearing down rather than building up.

Now more than ever, it is important for us to know that the coronavirus pandemic has highlighted the importance of getting youth and everyone involved in outdoor activities that can give us real life experiences.

As a result, we are happy to announce that heroes in our midst are sacrificing their time and resources and are affording youth the opportunity to go fishing, go walking in the woods, and see how many trees, wildflowers, and plants they can name. It is an exciting yet humbling experience to discover that the names of the many flowers, trees, and plants are seemingly too numerous to be counted, however each once of us volunteered to develop our individual catalog of names of plants and trees.

Many of us who have engaged in outdoor activities with youth soon discover that the youth, with their pride, are anxious to prove their physical prowess, especially endurance, against the older adults. The real challenge we older adults had was when we did not have the energy to keep up with the youth and their never-ending activities. I personally recalled telling a group of youth that I couldn't go any further. One of the youth looked at me with a condescending smile that led to a joking laugh as he said, "Why are you getting tired so quickly?"

I looked at him, smiled, and said, "Don't worry. When you get older, you will understand."

Several of the youth gave a thankful smile, and one said, "That's all right, mister. You are still our hero."

This is another example how challenges such as the coronavirus pandemic can be an impetus to encourage men and women in the community to join together on an ongoing basis and spend more time with our youth, even as we look beyond the pandemic's challenges.

The Day Our Sunday School Lesson Led Us to Talking about the Coronavirus Pandemic

Even before the coronavirus pandemic came on the scene, churches have been challenged with the declining participation of youth in Sunday school classes. Now, with the closure of local churches, it has exacerbated the challenge even more.

As an educator and a pastor, I have always placed special interest in introducing youth to the Bible and God through Sunday school classes. We must not forget it is our last best hope to help young people who are struggling to find meaning and purpose in life.

Tragically, our youth are not being afforded the opportunity to study the Scriptures in schools, and sadly even in some of our churches and homes. Therefore, they have not been given sufficient opportunities to discover for themselves who God is and develop a relationship with Him.

Because I am aware of this, especially in the midst of the coronavirus pandemic, I have develop several "satellite" Sunday school classes that will help give youths, and adults as well, a systematic way of seeking God via Bible study. One of my Sunday school classes in particular stands out because it led me and the participants to talking about the coronavirus.

It was not surprising to me because on this particular day, our Sunday school class centered on God, His creation, and what it tells us about who He is.

The Scripture reading for our Sunday school class was taken from the first chapter of John.

> In the beginning was the Word, and the Word was with God, and the Word was God. The same was in the beginning with God. All things were made by Him; and without Him was not anything made. (John 1:1–4 KJV)

Having done an extensive exegetical study on this passage before, I was aware I had to convey its meaning on a level that this predominantly youth class could relate to. Therefore, we focused on key words and phrases. There were two words that stood out in discussing the coronavirus in the form of a question from one of our youth. The youth asked, "If God is the Creator, why did He let this coronavirus thing happen?"

I knew from experience as a teacher that although I was not able to give a definitive answer, I must give an honest answer to the best of my ability. I said, "No one of us can know for sure, but what we do know is that as God allows things to happen, He intends for them to be for good in the end. Remember, we Christians are not exempt from sickness and disease because we are living in a world of sin. However, we have the assurance that He will never leave us or forsake us (Hebrews 13:5 KJV).

We can take comfort in knowing that He is in control. We are told in John 16:33 (KJV), "In the world you shall have tribulation: but be of good cheer; I have already overcome the world." We human beings do not fully know why God is allowing the coronavirus pandemic to happen, but one thing is for sure: He knows because He is the God who is omniscient (all-knowing), and He knows the beginning from the end."

It was not surprising this led into questions about the coronavirus.

One student asked, "Just what is the coronavirus?"

I replied, "Well, that is a good question. I can only tell you what the scientists tell us about it: According to the scientists, it is essentially a tiny bit of nucleic acids and protein that needs a living hosts. It is a respiratory virus. It can spread from person to person through droplets produced when an infected person coughs or sneezes. Also, it can remain on surfaces or objects and be transferred by touch and enter the human body through the mouth, nose, or eyes. Once inside the body, it begins infecting the glandular cells in the lining of the lungs."

"What are nucleic acids?" asked another student. As usual when teaching youth, one must always be ready for clarification questions in reply to your answer to their prior question.

It was becoming very clear that our dialoguing was going to be longer than I had anticipated. I said within I was glad that this was a satellite Sunday school Bible class, rather than a standard church Sunday school Bible study that was limited in time. With this in mind, I said, "Nucleic acids are macromolecules constructed from five elements: carbon, hydrogen, oxygen, nitrogen, and phosphorus. They play an important role in directing protein synthesis (formation). According to scientists, the two main classes of nucleic acids are deoxyribonucleic acid (DNA) and ribonucleic acid (RNA)."

"Wow! This is heavy stuff. You are using some big words. Pastor Charles, where did you learn all this?"

"In college, I learned a lot about this in my chemistry and biology classes. And as a public school teacher, the very nature of my job required me to read and research a lot."

"Who created all this stuff you talking about?" A student asked.

I realized this was a good question that could connect our discussion to our Sunday school Bible class. I knew this was a good opportunity to bring God back into the discussion. To answer the student's question, I said, "Remember that our Bible lesson today centers around John chapter one. We read in John 1:3 that all things were made by Him (GOD), and without Him was not anything made that was made. And we read in Acts 17:24 that God made the world and all things therein.

A student said, "Do you believe that all things were created by God?"

I replied, "Yes, because the Bible says so; although I know that most scientists do not agree with me. I am reminded of what I read in a science magazine several years ago. The topic was based on a question the scientist was trying to answer: How do cells know what to become? He talked about how DNA was formed. He expounded on his empirical evidence to show how cells are formed. However, his observation ended with a searching question. He said, 'The question I cannot answer is: How do cells know what to become?' As the scientist pondered on his question, he finally said, 'There must be some type of biological foreman in charge.' It is interesting how he stopped short of saying God is that biological foreman."

"Pastor Charles, we believe God is the Creator, and we believe He is who He says He is, and we believe in what the Bible says about Him," a student told me.

"We all can say amen to that."

Although it was time to end our class discussion, our youngest student anxiously held his hand up and asked a twofold question that none of us could fully answer. "What does a coronavirus look like? Is it some kind of alien or something?"

By now, everyone in the class seemed as if they had become oblivious to time, and they anxiously awaited my answer. I said, "I cannot tell you for sure, however with permission from my class, I will try to answer your question in a picture form." Everyone in the class nodded their heads. "You and I cannot see the coronavirus with our naked eye because it is very tiny.

Nevertheless, it is clear that we can see what it does. It is an enemy out to destroy us. However, if we use our imagination, we can picture who it is, give it a name, and give it shape and form.

"I invite you to join with me as we use our imagination and give the coronavirus a person-like name. Let's call the coronavirus the invisible soldier who is out to destroy us."

The Invisible Soldier

As I think of this invisible soldier, I think about the excitement of blowing soap bubbles into the air. Do you recall when you, as a child or when playing with your kids, blew soap bubbles from your hand? From the force of the air from our mouth, as we huff and puff, the soap bubbles at first take a large, spherical shape as they float through the air. Then the large bubbles burst into smaller bubbles, and the smaller bubbles burst into even smaller bubbles until they can no longer be seen with the naked eye, as they disappear into smaller molecules. Keep this picture in your mind because it will help explain how the coronavirus, the invisible soldier, operates.

Now picture with me as we describe the coronavirus as an invisible soldier, who is our enemy. We will now give it shape and form.

1. It has a round body that is loaded with acidic germs, which are his weapons of warfare used to kill people.
2. Its nearly round body looks like a spherically shaped ball. The spherical shape gives it a symmetrical balance that allows it to move in any direction with equal speed.

How does it attack us: Its method of attack is accomplished by hitchhiking on involuntary human hosts. It means that each one of us can be chosen as his hosts to carry its deadly virus, a combination of nucleic acid and proteins.

It can spread from host to host as each host coughs or sneezes, discharging the little invisible soldiers that float through the air as its larger bubbles explode into smaller and smaller bubbles and finally into the form of tiny molecules.

It enters into the human hosts through their eyes, mouth, or nose. Once inside the body of a human host, it attaches itself to the outer layers of the humans cells, infects the respiratory system, and begins multiplying. Once it reaches the lower respiratory system of a human host, it can cause death.

It is important to remember the coronavirus, the invisible soldier, can be transferred by a human host who touches the surface of objects that have been contaminated with droplets of the virus. And remember that although a host may be asymptomatic, one can still be a carrier of this communicable virus.

When I was done explaining, an older student said, "Wow! This is scary stuff. What makes it more dangerous is that the coronavirus, this invisible enemy soldier, cannot be seen with our naked eye. Thanks for helping us use our imagination to give it a three-dimensional shape and form, to help us visualize it better. I have one final question: What can we do to help defeat the coronavirus, now that we are able to visualize it in a physical sense?"

I replied, "That is a good question. Remember that in any type of war, we must first of all know who our enemy is, how it operates, and what kind of weapons does it use. We have already discovered that this invisible enemy uses biological germs for it weapons. And we have already discussed that it uses human hosts as it hitchhikes onto them and uses them to spread its little but deadly invisible soldiers from person to person or object to object. Once it reaches the inside of a human, it multiples in the human body and can cause death.

An older student said, "That is frightening, but what can we do to defeat these invisible soldiers?"

"That is another good question. First of all, we Christians

must remember we are in the army of the Lord, and He has never lost a battle. Having said that, let us remember we cannot defeat this invisible soldier by retreating behind four walls and hoping these invisible soldiers will soon end their siege and go away. We must go on the attack, but with the right weapons. First, know that prayer is our number one weapon, because in prayer we are dialoguing with God, and He will direct our paths. Second, He has given scientists the knowledge and ability to develop weapons that can help us defend against this enemy—weapons such as disinfectants, antibacterial solutions, and medical protective items such as gloves, body suits, and face masks. But notice that I have only listed weapons we can use externally or topically. Next, I am going to mention the most effective way to defeat this invisible enemy."

Developing and Using a Weapon That Can Go Inside the Human Body and Fight the Invisible Soldier, the Coronavirus

I continued my discussion. "Remember that we said the invisible soldier, the coronavirus, does it real damage when it gets inside the human body. So the question is, How do we figure out a way to develop invisible soldiers to go inside the human body and destroy the invisible enemy?"

Immediately, I realized that with that question, I had struck the inner chord of one of my young student's imagination. He was so filled with excitement because he had an answer, and he made a noise as he frantically raised his hands in the air. I gestured toward him with a receptive nod, and he said, "That means we've got to develop invisible soldiers to go inside the human body and destroy the invisible enemy soldiers that have invaded it."

I gave a big, affirming smile and said to the young student, "You've got the right idea. It sounds like you are going to be a scientist one day. Perhaps one day, you will be a scientist for the Lord."

"Yes. With God's blessing, I will study and become a scientist one day."

"I believe you will do well in the science field. But the point I want to make to each one of you today is this: That is essentially what the US government, the private sector, the pharmaceutical companies, and the scientists are doing in their process of developing a vaccine shot that can be injected into the human body, to destroy the invisible enemy soldiers that enter into it. Also, may we never forget that God has already made, inside our bodies, millions and billions of cells that make our bodies immune to other diseases and germs. However, we must keep in mind that once our autoimmune system weakens, it can no longer effectively fight of diseases such as the coronavirus.

"Let us give President Trump and his administration, the private sector, the pharmaceutical companies, and the scientists and doctors thanks for their miraculous work during Operation Warp Speed, developing a vaccine to stop the killing effect of the coronavirus. Surely we know it is God who made it possible. Let all say amen to this.

"Meanwhile, listen to what God is telling us in the midst of the coronavirus pandemic. Use the gifts and resources that God has given you to help others. Show gratitude for those who are on the front lines in our communities on a daily basis—and yes, do not forget to give our young people kudos for their job well done. First and foremost, be thankful and pray to God for His protection and His watching over us." We ended our Sunday school class and discussion of the coronavirus with a prayer.

The youngest student said, "This has been a good day. The entire class said, "Amen."

Observing and Dialoguing with Doctors, Nurses, and Other Medical Assistants

When we think of heroes on the front lines, I am sure you will agree with me that our doctors, nurses, and other medical related personnel are on the extreme front lines. I have had firsthand experience in seeing upfront the immeasurable roles that our medical personnel play.

The main reason I can attest to this fact is because I in general, and as a clergy, have observed and dialogued with our medical personnel taking on the challenge of rendering medical and health services in the midst of the coronavirus pandemic, as well as other emergency events.

As I observed them in action, it once again reminded me that most often, our greatest ministry is done on the outside of the walls of a local church. No other event in my memory better drives home this point than the coronavirus pandemic.

In the midst of the coronavirus pandemic, I have come to realize this also applies to Christians. Think about it: Due to the mandate of the government and state officials, local churches were closed and therefore had to use alternative methods to reach their congregants and the people in the community.

Case in point, as I pondered on the challenges that our churches were facing as a result of local churches' closures, I kept hearing a quiet, still voice within me saying, "Now that the local churches are closed, will you still serve me?"

Suddenly, I realized it was God asking me this question. And without hesitating, I answered, "Yes, Lord."

Needless to say, it did not take long for me to find out whether or not I was able to walk the walk, so to speak.

The real test came in the early part of 2020, when hospitals and doctors were no longer accepting patients or doing routine operations. Only emergency medical needs were being met. In the midst of the near shutdown of our hospitals, I was soon put to the test. It dawn on me that I too, as a clergy, am on call twenty-four hours a day, coronavirus or no coronavirus. And may I never forget where there is a need, there is a ministry opportunity.

A phone call I received one late night in April 2020 reminded me of this very point. As the phone began ringing, I grudgingly awoke from my sleep and answered the phone. "Hello, who is calling?"

"Pastor Charles, Pastor Charles! This is Sister Jones, one of your former church members. I have fallen in my house and cannot get up. I tried calling others, but no one answered their phone."

I quickly said, "Sister Jones, are you in pain?"

"Yes, I feel pain above my right knee."

"Sister Jones, please stay where you are. Do not try to get up. I will dial 911 and request an emergency ambulance to go to your house as soon as possible. Meanwhile, stay where you are. Do not try to get up, because you might injure yourself further. I will be at your house in a few minutes. In the meantime, remember God is with you, and He will work out everything for good."

"Thank you, Pastor Charles. With God's help and your help, I know I will be all right," she replied.

I quickly called 911, and after identifying myself, I reported that Sister Jones, an elderly lady, had fallen in her house and was unable to get up. I indicated to them that she might have broken her upper right leg. After I gave them her address, they promised they would call the emergency service ambulance personnel to dispatch someone to her house as soon as possible. In reply, I said, "Thank you, I will be there waiting on them."

Five minutes after I arrived at Sister Jones's house, the emergency ambulance crew arrived, along with two policemen in their car. Fortunately, they were able to manipulate one of the doors to Sister Jones's house and enter.

We found her lying on the floor. After a preliminary examination, they said it appeared she had broken her leg in the area above her right knee, and they would take her to the emergency room.

After helping Sister Jones locate her purse and necessary medical records, along with phone numbers of some of her family members, I gave the emergency personnel her medical records and her insurance cards. Shortly thereafter, they loaded her onto a stretcher and put her in the ambulance. I reminded them I would accompany her to the hospital in my personal car, and I would also try to get in touch with some member of her family.

As a clergy, I have seen this occurrence happen to some of our elderly citizens time and again. It is a sad fact that many elderly people who live alone often do not have family members nearby and thereby must depend on their pastor or clergy, or others, in times of an emergency.

As for me, It was another reminder that my ministry is not constrained by the walls of a local church. Anytime I doubt what serving others means, I always remember what Jesus says in Matthew 25:40 (KJV): "In as much you have served the least of them, you have served me."

I was finally able to locate one of Sister Jones's close relatives who was at work. He indicated that as soon as he could get off work, he would meet us at the hospital.

Upon arriving at the hospital with the emergency service ambulance and checking Sister Jones into an emergency room, I said thanks to the ambulance driver and assistant. With smiles on their faces, they indicated to me they were just doing their job.

Suddenly a little voice within said, "Don't let them get away without saying how important their service is."

I got their attention and said, "I want each one of you to know that working as first responders means you are indeed heroes of a special kind."

With smiles on their faces, they responded, "Thank you for that, but we are just doing what we are supposed to do."

Needless to say, this ordeal led me to the hospital, where

I could see firsthand the great work and ministry our medical personnel were rendering in our hospitals, especially in the midst of the coronavirus pandemic. It was determined by the doctors that Sister Jones had a fracture in her right leg just above her knee. After her successful operation, she was assigned several weeks of rehabilitation, with a follow-up appointment to visit an orthopedic doctor.

As a result of Sister Jones and other senior citizens who had ongoing medical challenges, I volunteered, and in some cases was drafted, to accompany or personally transport them to the hospital. I soon became a familiar face in the local hospitals. Because people knew that I was a clergy, I was afforded the opportunity to go in restricted areas that regular visitors could not normally access. As a clergy, I have always believed that God has His walls of protection around me. With this in mind, I often went where others dared not tread.

One of the visits that stands out in my memory is when I accompanied Sister Jones to the orthopedic center.

Observing and Dialoguing with a Doctor, Nurses, and Other Medical Personnel in the Orthopedic Center

Upon entering the orthopedic center's waiting room and making sure Sister Jones was signed in, the few of us in the waiting room sat in seats that were spaced at least six feet apart. Shortly thereafter, Sister Jones's name was called by one of the X-ray technicians.

After taking Sister Jones to the X-ray room, the technician soon returned to the waiting room and mentioned that Sister Jones had reminded her I was her pastor. With a look of assurance on her face, she asked me to please come into the X-ray room.

After entering the X-ray room, I soon discovered that due to the shortage of assistants, she had no one to help her lift Sister

Jones, whom I estimated to weigh at least two hundred pounds. I recognized she needed help in removing Sister Jones from the wheelchair onto the X-ray table. She somewhat apologetically asked me to assist her. "Oh course," I said. "I will be more than happy to do so."

After the two of us managed to safely lift Sister Jones onto the X-ray table, the technician smiled and thanked me. "Sure, I said, I will wait outside the X-ray room while you are taking images of her right leg."

"Okay," she said. "I will call you as soon as the X-rays are completed."

While waiting outside, I recalled what the Scripture says about being ready to serve one another humbly in love (Galatians 5:13).

Shortly thereafter, the X-ray technician invited me to return to the X-ray room said, "Thanks for your help."

I quickly replied, "You are welcome. I am honored to be of assistance." Now it was my time to show appreciation to the technician for her service. "Thank you for your service. I want you to know that you are a hero, and your job is ever so important."

"Wow! I never considered myself to be a hero. How so?" she asked.

"Here is how: You are doing what heroes do. You are allowing God to use your skills to help others in time of need."

Sister Jones and I were soon in the doctor's office, waiting for the orthopedic evaluation and recommendation.

Observing and Dialoguing with a Nurse/Pastor

Prior to the doctor doing the orthopedic evaluation and recommendation, a male nurse assistant came in and greeted us as he prepared to check Sister Jones's vital signs. "Good morning. I am the assistant nurse assigned to check the patient's vital signs."

Sister Jones had an anxious look on her face and said, "Good morning, nurse. I hope you will find that my checkup will be okay."

With a compassionate smile on his face, he said, "I am sure everything will be all right."

I then introduced myself. "Good morning, nurse. My name is Pastor Charles, and I am accompanying Sister Jones today. This is my way of ministering outside the walls of the local church."

With a broad smile on his face, he said, "It is a pleasure meeting you. By the way, I am bi-vocational, in that I am a pastor in one of the local churches in one of the nearby towns. At the same time, I work here in the hospital as a nurse. So you can call me Pastor Johnson or Nurse Johnson, whichever one you feel more comfortable with."

I responded, "Although I am keenly aware that your title as pastor is to be respected, in line with your nurse duties in the hospital, I will appropriately call you Nurse Johnson."

"Thank you, Pastor Charles. And I notice that you are serving on the outside of the walls of a local church, also, in that you are accompanying Sister Jones and helping her take care of her medical appointments."

I said, "Yes, and may I remind you what God has told me in the midst of the coronavirus pandemic."

With an inquisitive look on his face, Nurse Johnson said, "Yes, please do."

I gave a solemn smile and I said, "Here is what God said to me: 'Now that I have closed the doors of local churches will you still serve me?'"

With a special countenance on his face, Nurse Johnson said, "Thanks for that powerful affirmation Now I know that is what He has been asking me."

I chuckled with an affirmative gesture. "It appears that is what you are doing right now, in that you are not only serving as a pastor of a local church, but you are also serving in the ministry of nursing outside the walls of a local church."

"Yes, that is true. Although I never thought of it in the way you described it. But it describes who I am. Although I am a bi-vocational pastor, my service on the outside of a local church has reminded me that our ministry reaches outside the walls of a church."

I smiled and said, "I think you and I are on the same wavelength, listening to the voice of God."

"Pastor Charles, that reminds me of what I told one of my older members a few days ago. She had called me concerned that because her local church is closed due to the coronavirus pandemic. As a result, she felt as if she was not serving the Lord, because she could not go to church every Sunday. Using my pastoral insight, I reminded her in an encouraging way by telling her she could also serve the Lord by praying, reading the Bible, and helping others on the outside of her local church. I told her to remember when the time is right in the eyes of the Lord, He will reopen the doors of local churches again. She replied by saying, 'Thanks, Pastor Johnson. I needed that. I have been feeling guilty because I could not attend church every Sunday.'"

Pastor Johnson continued. "I told her, 'Sister, always remember you can serve the Lord wherever you are. When you allow this to happen, you can be a servant for God and others.'"

I told Nurse Johnson in an affirming way, "I want you to know that you are a hero in many ways, because you serve as a pastor, as well as a nurse. May God bless you in all your endeavors."

Nurse Johnson replied, "Thank you for those encouraging words." Then he realized we had dialogued so much that he was beginning to neglect his duty as a nurse. As he looked at his watch, he said, "Oops, I am running behind on my schedule. Pastor Charles, it is a blessing to have dialogued with you." After we exchanged business cards, he said, "May God bless you in all your endeavors."

I responded, "Likewise. May God bless you too."

As he prepared to leave, he said in a sincere voice, "Thank

you for your service. And remember, Pastor Charles, you are a hero in so many ways."

Observing and Dialoguing with a Doctor

The doctor soon entered and said, "Please forgive me for keeping you waiting. One of my patients was experiencing some medical challenges."

I responded, "Doctor, that is quite all right. I understand that you, as an orthopedic doctor, are especially busy during the surge of the coronavirus pandemic, and that your patients primarily come through the emergency service." Then I smiled and added, "By the way, we were left alone for only a few minutes. Nurse Johnson, whom I also found out is a pastor in one of our local churches, showed great compassion with Sister Jones as he checked her vital signs. We also had a good dialogue about the importance of ministering outside our local churches."

With an accommodating smile on his face, the doctor said, "I am Doctor Price, Sister Jones's orthopedic doctor."

Sister Jones responded, "Good morning, Doctor. I want you to meet Pastor Charles, who has been so kind to me by bringing me to see you today."

Doctor Price said, "Pleased to meet you too. I heard that you are a minister. I am sure you and Nurse Johnson had a good dialogue."

I nodded and said, "Yes, it was a pleasure talking with him."

Doctor Price took this opportunity to remind us that Nurse Johnson was quite an asset in the hospital. "He not only shows a lot of compassion in working with our patients as a nurse, but he also is a very valuable spiritual counsel, which I think is helpful for our patients' healing process." In refocusing his attention on Sister Jones, his patient, he said, "I checked the X-rays of your leg, and it indicates your leg seems to be healing okay. According to the nurse report, your vital signs appears to be near or within the normal range. However, I am going to recommend that you continue receiving physical therapy for another two weeks, after which you will need to see me again. Also, I am going to send in a prescription for medication. Again, I am pleased with your progress."

With a smile on her face, Sister Jones said, "Thank you, doctor."

As Doctor Price looked in my direction, I seized the moment to make sure I did not forget to say thanks to him. "I thank you also for the wonderful work you are doing. And by the way, Doctor, I want you to know and the other doctors, nurses, and medical workers to know I think you are doing great work during the coronavirus pandemic, and at all times. You have a special ministry."

Doctor Price gave a grateful smile and said, "I thank you for those fine commendations. I do not consider myself to be a minister, but I do try to be a good Christian."

I said, "Well, please remember that God has given all of us gifts to use in a ministry that reach outside the local church. Yours is ever so important in that you are in the health and healing ministry of men and women. And may I add you all are among our greatest heroes, in that you all are on the front lines every day in your service. So I thank you for being a special hero for God and others."

"Thank you, Pastor Charles, and may I remind you that you are doing heroic works also in helping to serve the whole person, spiritually as well as physically," responded Dr. Price. "Have a good day," he said as he hurried to see his next patient.

Dialoguing with a Policeman Who Is
Also a Former Military Veteran

As I was driving Sister Jones back to her home, I saw the flashing lights of a police car. It appeared the policeman had pulled someone over and was going through his routine checkup. I did not stop to see why, but I said to myself, "The policeman is doing his duties, upholding the traffic and safety laws."

It reminded me that our law enforcement officers are getting a bad rap from much of the public. There is a segment of people in our society who are unappreciative of the work the men and women of law enforcement perform night and day to keep our cities and communities safe and secure.

As a minster of the Gospel, I am reminded of what God says about leaders and those in authority in Romans 13.

> Everyone must submit himself to the government authorities, for there is no authority except that which God has established. The authorities that exist have been established by God. Consequently, he who rebels against the authority is rebelling against what God has instituted, and those who do so will bring judgement on themselves. For rulers hold no terror for those who do right, but for those who do wrong. Do you want to be free from fear of the one in authority? Then do what is right and he will commend you. For he is God's servant to do you good. But if you do wrong, be afraid, for he does not bear the sword for nothing. He is God's servant, an agent of wrath to bring punishment on the wrongdoer. Therefore, it is necessary to submit to authorities, not only because of possible punishment but also because of conscience. (Romans 13:1–5 NIV)

As I reflected on this, a fellow military veteran who now is serving as a police officer came to my mind. I will call him Sgt. Mack. He stands out in my mind because over the years, I have had the privilege of knowing him personally, and I have observed him in the line of duty as a police officer. In addition, I aware that he is well-known for his involvement in his local community activities as he strives to encourage people to work together for the common good of all. The overwhelming majority of people whom I know in my community have great respect and appreciation for this officer.

I pondered on why some people hate police officers and tend to blame them for the ills of our society. I asked myself why this negative attitude toward law enforcement agents was prevailing. Is it because some in our society think law and order enforcement are not administered equitably? Is it because many in our society do not want to follow a standard set of rules for the common good of our society? Is it because the attitude begins with not having the proper reverential fear, or respect for God, and it therefore trickles down through every level of authority in our society—parents, clergy, teachers, policeman, and so on? Is it because many in our society do not understand that without law and order, a civilized society becomes a disordered society? Is it because the disruption of law and order is sometimes used to achieve a political agenda or some other self-serving motive? Is it because many in our society do not understand that human rights, human responsibility, and human accountability are entwined, and in the scheme of freedom, all three of these components must work together in a balanced way?

Whatever the cause, it is very clear that the police and other law enforcement officers have been unwittingly used as scapegoats for the disruption of law and order in our society.

I am sure you will agree with me on this one thing: If you are fighting a war, and you want to know what is going on in a war, invariably you must talk with the foot soldiers who have their boots on the ground.

Case in point, if one wants to know what's going on in our cities and towns in terms of law enforcement, one must dialogue with the police and other law enforcements officers who patrol and walk in our community night and day.

With this in mind, one of the best ways to get answers to some of these questions was to talk to Sgt Mack, a well-respected policeman in our town.

A few days after pondering on this, I was able to talk with him while he was on duty and in his patrol car near the courthouse. I made sure I was not interrupting his routine duties, approached his patrol car, and greeted him. "Sgt. Mack, how are you doing today? I hope I am not interfering with your job."

He quickly recognized me and said, "Pastor Charles, it is good to see you again. How are you doing?"

"I am doing well. How are you doing?" I asked.

He responded, "I am doing well too. What can I do for you today?"

"I would like to set up an appointment to meet with you when you are of duty," I replied.

With a smile on his face, he joked, "What are you going to preach to me about this time?"

"Well, to make a long story short, it is not about preaching this time. Rather, it has been on my mind to meet with you, say thanks in a personal way for your service as a policeman, and dialogue with you about what it means to be a policeman nowadays."

He replied, "Thanks. I could use some encouragement. And knowing that you are a man of God, it will be a pleasure talking with you about this, especially knowing that you are also a military veteran as I am, and you served as a military policeman while in service. Clearly, we have a lot in common. I look forward to talking with you. Call me around eight this evening, and we will take it from there."

After calling Sgt. Mack, we arranged to meet at 8:30 p.m. When I arrived at his house, Mrs. Mack answered the door. After greeting Mrs. Mack and taking care of all the introductory protocols, I began dialoguing with Sgt. Mack. I said, "I must confess, I have never seen so much hate against police officers and other law enforcement authorities as we are witnessing these days. My spiritual discernment tells me that it is more far-reaching then just hating the law enforcement personnel. It is a hate that is permeating our entire society. Our police officers are getting the brunt of it, because you all are on the front line of enforcing law and order. In particular, I want to encourage you today by letting you know that you guys and gals are getting blame for something that is deeper than law and order."

Sgt. Mack gave a sigh of relief after hearing this. He said, "This takes a heavy load off my shoulders, knowing that we are not the sole blame for the unrest in our society. Pastor Charles, I have always enjoyed talking with you because you seem to be able to look at life with a broad perspective, rather than the narrow and biased perspective that is prevailing in our society today."

At this juncture, I immediately recognized that I must let Sgt. Mack know that he too had a broad perspective on life, and that he was very capable of dialoguing with a give and take attitude. I quickly reminded him, "It is no accident that you and I can talk in a civil way, because we both learn from each other. After dialoguing with each other, we both end up becoming stronger in our belief that there still is a chance to make this world a better in which to live, no matter what challenges lie ahead, although neither of us has all the answers.

"I am reminded when, in my younger days, I did not realize I was naïve in so many ways. I thought I had all the answers. One day, my father set the record straight as we were dialoguing with one another. It happened because for everything he mentioned, I had the attitude that I always had the correct answers. He said something to me that I will never forget. My father had a pointed look in his eyes and said, 'Let me tell you something, boy! When a person thinks he has all the answers, it is obvious he does not have all the questions.' I always try to remember this when I am dialoguing with someone."

After hearing me make that statement, Sgt. Mack gave out

an affirming chuckle. "That has a lot of truth in it. I am going to record it in my memory bank." Then he got a more serious look on his face as he entered into deep thought. He eventually asked, "What do you think is causing so much unrest in our society?"

> A quote by John Adams, America's second president, came to my mind, and I quoted it to him: "Our constitution was made only for a moral and religious people, It is wholly inadequate to the government of any other."

After hearing that statement, Sgt. Mack sprang from his chair as if he had been jolted by an invisible force. As he stood up with his hands in the air, he said in a loud voice, "Pastor Charles, you are preaching now!"

I gave an affirming smile while trying to control my own emotions, and after realizing I had touched on a truth that speaks to us in a resounding way, I said, "Surely I believe you and I can agree John Adams's statement is speaking to us today with an urgent reminder. In fact, according the Pew Research Center, in the United State, the decline of Christianity affiliation continues at a rapid rate, and the increase of 'nonreligious affiliation is rising."

Sgt. Mack replied, "Does this mean that we in America, and our society in general, are moving further away from religious and moral restraints?"

"Short of a religious revival happening soon, the answer is yes," I answered.

"Pastor Charles, based on our dialogue so far, I am sure you agree with me that this explains why America is becoming less civilized each day."

"Yes, I said. "It is a logical conclusion when we understand that as we lose our moral and religious compass, we will also lose our Christian standards, and consequently our civility will decline. As a result, people will begin doing that which they think is right in their own minds."

Sgt. Mack had a solemn look on his face. "This helps explain why we policemen and other law enforcement personnel see our jobs becoming more challenging."

"Yes, and may I say at this juncture that as a former military policeman in the US armed forces, I can empathize with you as a civilian policeman, because I can identify with certain nuances that make a police officer's job more difficult."

"How so?" Sgt. Mack asked.

"For example, how many times have you arrested or attempted to arrest someone who has become legally drunk on alcohol or high on drugs?" I asked.

Sgt. Mack answered, "Oh, my, too many times for me to remember."

"The point I want to make by asking that question is that you and I know from experience when law enforcement officers are trying to detain or arrest a person under this condition, we often find that it can be extremely difficult and often dangerous."

Sgt. Mack understood what I was talking about. "You got that right. One thing I am sure you, as a former military policeman, found out is that people under the influence of alcohol or drugs also lose much of their inhibitions, and as a consequence, they lose their ability to reason or control their own emotions or strength. Pastor Charles, when you were a policeman, did you ever encounter people like that when trying to detain or arrest them?"

After laughing for a while, I said, "You'd better believe it. I can still remember some of these encounters as if they happened just yesterday. "And you know something? I am going to be frank: there were times when I feared for my safety."

After hearing me make this statement, Sgt. Mack gave a big smile and looked around, making sure no one else was looking or listening. He said, "Me too, but don't tell anybody I said this."

"Sgt. Mack, there is so much more you and I could talk about, but there is one thing I want to share with you. You police officers have one of the most important ministries in our society, and that is enforcing law and order. For without the great work done by men and women like you, we could not maintain a civilized society. Remember that when no one seems to appreciate the special job that you and your fellow law enforcement personnel are doing every day and night, and when you are experiencing increasing challenges, so much so that you sometimes feel like giving up. Remember that you serve a greater cause than the job itself. You are God's servant. God will keep His walls of protection around you and His guardian angels in charge over you. And again, thanks for your service in the US military and your current service as a policeman. Whether people recognize it or not, I say you are a hero in so many ways. May God bless you each and every day."

Thanks, I needed that. Also, I want to thank you for your military service, and your service in the Gospel ministry. Pastor Charles, keep on being a hero for God and others. May God bless you in all your endeavors. Be safe!"

Chapter 7

If God Is a Loving God, Why Does He Allow Suffering?

Often I am asked the question, "If God is a loving God, why does He allow suffering?" I always find it necessary to define the word *suffering*.

For the purpose of writing on this all-encompassing question, the Oxford English Dictionary gives one of the best and simplest definitions: "The state of undergoing pain, distress or hardship."

We all can agree that the coronavirus pandemic has caused pain, distress, and hardship, either directly or indirectly, in everyone's lives.

In the midst of the coronavirus spreading throughout the United States, it has been estimated by experts that two hundred or more countries and territories worldwide are experiencing the effects of the pandemic. Consequently, people are experiencing much fear and hopelessness as they endure pain, distress, despair, and hardship.

May we choose to remember that even in the midst of pain, even in the midst of distress, and even in the midst of despair, hardship, and challenges, God is still in control, and surely He will keep His word. In Isaiah 41:10 (NLT), God reminds us, "Don't be afraid, for I am with you. Do not be dismayed, for I am your

God. I will strengthen you. I will help you. I will uphold you with my victorious right hand."

Often I am asked by Christians, "Why does God allow this disease to affect Christians?" Oh course, no one can give a definitive answer, but what we can say is that Christians are not exempt from sickness and diseases because we live in a world of sin. However, we as Christians can take comfort in knowing that God can prevent or heal all manner of sickness, according to His will., Again remember what He says in the Scripture: "In this world you shall have tribulation: but be of good cheer; I have overcome the world" (John 16:33 KJV). In Hebrews 13:5, He tells us that He will never leave us or forsake us.

However, I am aware there are still many who ask questions: If God is a loving God, why does it seems like He does not care? If God is in control, why does He allow so much suffering to happen? And if God is so powerful, why is He not able to stop all the suffering?

In fact, I am often asked about suffering. Why does God allow evil acts to occur? I do not fully know, for it is a mystery to us as to why. However, I can assure you of this one thing: When God allows suffering to happen, it is ultimately for our good.

We must remember that God has made everything for His purpose. Listen to what He says in Proverbs: "The LORD has made everything for His purpose, even the wicked for the day of trouble" (Proverbs 16:4 NASB).

In my opinion, one of the best answers to the question as to why God allows evil acts to happen comes from a wise old preacher whose name remains anonymous. Here is what I recalled him saying in answer to the question about evil: "God sometimes allows evil to happen in order to show how much He loves us."

Of course I am very aware that one could counter, "If God is love, why does He have to allow evil to happen in order to prove He loves us?" To answer this question, I believe it is important to look at several biblical reasons why God allows suffering.

1. Suffering is the result of humankind's sin. Sin entered into world because humankind chose to reject God's command. As a result humans have suffered ever since (see Genesis 3).
2. A person sometimes suffers because of wrong choices made by oneself or other human beings. The good news: God can use this suffering for good (Genesis 50:20).
3. Suffering provides us an opportunity to comfort one another (2 Corinthians 1:3–4).
4. God sometimes allows us to suffer in order to test our faith or determine our trust in Him (see the book of Job).
5. God allows us to suffer in order to get us to turn to Him in repentance rather than perish for eternity (Luke 13:1–4).
6. God disciplines the ones He loves (Hebrews 12:6–11).
7. God sometimes allows us to suffer so we can come to the end of "self," so that we can see God for who He is and turn to Him with every aspect of our lives (Luke 15:11–32).
8. In suffering there is a message of warning. It is a message for all of us. He is reminding each one of us it is a time to have a sense of urgency. We all need to be very sure we are prepared for our eternal future by inviting God into our lives right now, for tomorrow is not promised to us (James 4:13–14).

There is no single answer to why God allows suffering. However, for those of us who have even a cursory knowledge of the Bible are aware that suffering for humankind has been around since the disobedience in the Garden of Eden, and it will be around until Christ returns.

As we struggle for the answer to suffering, we can take comfort in knowing that the Bible provides us a biblical perspective on suffering, that which can give us hope even in the midst of suffering.

And remember: the good news is the Bible tells us innocent suffering is redemptive. He is not only working all things for good; He also tells us in Scripture there is a great reward waiting for us in heaven, that which will make up for every loss here on earth a thousandfold over (2 Corinthians 4:16–18).

By looking at the biblical reasons for suffering, I am sure we all agree that even in the midst of suffering, we can have hope. However, we must be aware that the world teaches us to blame others for our suffering.

A word of caution: May we never fall into the trap of playing the blame game for our suffering or our mistakes, because it is a no-win approach to alleviating suffering and setbacks in life.

The Danger of Playing the Blame Game for the Reason of Our Suffering

In the midst of the coronavirus pandemic, we find many people using it as a reason to play the blame game. Unfortunately, in some cases it is used for the purpose of gaining political advantage. And for others, it is being used as a means of promoting the attitude of victimization.

Consequently, there are some in our midst hitchhiking on the coronavirus pandemic suffering as a means to blame others for their conceived suffering in other areas of life.

The danger in using the blame game is that it is a way of blaming others for our suffering or unfavorable circumstance rather than accepting our individual responsibility. Often this approach is called passing the buck.

The best approach that each one of us should take in the midst of suffering, or any unfavorable circumstance, is to remember that each one of us is called on to do our individual part in comforting, aiding and supporting one another along the way.

When I think of the blame game, I am reminded of the sour grapes in Aesop's Fables, which used it to signify resentment.

However, the Scriptures give us a historical implication of the misuse of the sour grapes theory.

The Day God Nullified the Sour Grape Theory

In ancient Israel, the sour grapes theory was used as a proverb by the people to excuse themselves by saying they were being punished for the sins of their forefathers (Lamentations 5:7; see also Jeremiah 31:29–31).

Think about it, the proverb was used in a way to provide an excuse for their suffering by placing the blame on their parents or forefathers. In essence, it was a way of saying it was not because of the sins of the present groups but because of their fathers' or forefathers' guilt.

Speaking through Ezekiel, God set the record straight, and He nullified the sour grapes theory in Ezekiel 18.

The word of the Lord came to me:

> What do you mean by repeating this proverb concerning the land of Israel, "The parents have eaten sour grapes, and the children's teeth are set on edge?"

> As I live says the LORD God, this proverb shall no more be used by you in Israel.

> Know that all lives are mine; the life of the parents as well as the life of the child is mine: It is only the person who sins shall die. (Ezekiel 18:1–4 KJV)

These passages speak volume to us today. It is vanity to play the blame game. It is vanity today to try to use the sour grapes theory in an attempt to blame others for our suffering, or to blame others for our claim of victimization.

Each one of us must remember that our current state of suffering cannot simply be blamed on others; rather, each one has to carry one's own responsibility, with its subsequent accountability.

And so let us awaken from our self-pity party, rise up, and take individual responsibility for helping each other overcome suffering in every aspect of our lives. When we allow this to happen, our lives will take on a new meaning. We will begin to understand that we serve a greater cause than the self, even in the midst of suffering.

When we allow this to happen, we will discover that heroes from every walk of life are in our midst, and that we too can be heroes for God and for others. Remember: With God on our side, we are more than conquerors (Romans 8:37).

Chapter 8

We Have Much to Be Thankful for, Even in the Midst of Suffering

Why is it so difficult in our society to exercise a prevailing attitude of thankfulness?

Although I have said it before, it is worth repeating. In part, it is because we live in a society that is primarily driven by the ideal of self-centeredness, that which focuses on me, myself, and I, which is described as individualism.

However, one thing that we should be learning from our suffering in the midst of the coronavirus pandemic is that no person is an island unto oneself. God has a way of letting us know that we are created as relational beings; we are created to be relational to God and human beings. And we need each other in order for our basic needs as well as others' needs to be met. Surely the coronavirus pandemic is reminding us of this very fact.

Let me refresh your memory by restating the six basic levels of human needs: physical needs, security needs, social needs, self-esteem needs, self-actualization needs, and spiritual self-actualization needs. When we realize none of these needs can be met without God and others, we can begin to be infused with an attitude of gratitude, that is, thankfulness. We can be thankful to God for the heroes in our lives, and for using us to be heroes.

We must not allow ourselves to become so self-centered, believing that we are responsible for all that is good in our lives, while at the same time blaming others for the suffering that we encounter in our daily life. Only when we humble ourselves and develop the discipline of gratitude can we begin to recognize that God is in control and that we can rely on Him for meeting our needs in good or bad times.

I know some of you who are reading this and are still saying, "You sound so convincing and encouraging, but you do not realize the pain, distress, and hardship I am going through right now. How can I be thankful when I have lost my job? How can I be thankful when my mother is in the hospital, not expecting to live? How can I be thankful when I have no money to pay my bills or put food on the table? How can I be thankful when it seems like my world is falling apart?"

For those who feel this way, I hear you. I can hear your sense of hopelessness. This is the way the world would have you to think under these circumstances. But I have an answer from the one who created the whole universe and everything therein (Acts 17:24), and as He says through Apostle Paul, "Give thanks *in all circumstances*, for this is God's will for you in Christ Jesus" (1 Thessalonians 5:18 NIV).

Notice I emphasized the words *in all circumstances*. The point I want to make is that Paul, through the inspiration of God, is not telling us to be thankful for these things; rather we are to be thankful in all our circumstances. In reading 1 Thessalonians 5:18, it once again shows how important it is to know the meaning of the little prepositional words such as *in* and *for* in biblical verses. It can make a big difference how we interpret the true meaning and implication of a passage or verse, in the context that it is used.

For example, it is a big difference between being thankful *for* every situation in life as opposed to being thankful *in* those situations. Paul is reminding us to be thankful in all aspects of our life, both good or bad, knowing that whatever God allows to happen it is for the ultimate good.

Oh, if we only would take time out and reflect on what is happening around us that we take for granted. Then we would begin to understand that even in the midst of suffering, we have so much to be thankful for. We can be thankful for a God who loves us, thankful for a sovereign God who is too wise to make a mistake and too powerful to fail, and thankful for a God who keeps His promises. Or we can simply think Him for the many things we take for granted, seen and unseen—millions upon millions of things, like the air we breathe, the food we eat, and more. And yes, we can be thankful for the many heroes He places in our midst.

Paul goes on to tell us in the Scripture that God is able to make all things, the good, the bad, and everything in between, to work out for good: "And we know that *in all things* God works for the good of those who love Him" (Romans 8:28 NIV; *emphasis added*). Notice that this verse does not say *for all things*; rather, it says *in all things*, echoing what is said in 1 Thessalonians 5:18 (KJV).

It is wonderful to know that no matter what we are going through—the coronavirus pandemic, or whatever comes our way—God is using it for the ultimate good for those who love Him. It means we win in the end no matter what comes our way, because God knows what is best for us. And He is able to keep His promises. This, in and of itself, is enough to be thankful for.

But the question still remains: How is America expressing its thanksgiving?

How Is America Expressing Its Thanksgiving, or Lack of Thanksgiving, Even in the Midst of the Coronavirus Pandemic?

As I said earlier, our society has taught us to place much emphasis on the ideal of individualism, and as a result, it has spawned the attitude that whatever we have achieved or whatever is given to us, it is because we, as individuals, have earned it or have an entitlement to receive it because of who we are.

While each individual life is important, we must remember that the concept of individualism means when a person is controlled by a self-centered approach or conduct, it can cause a person to pursue one's own ends for one's own good, rather than the common good of all.

The challenge that the concept of individualism faces is that it cannot operate in the mode of love as commanded by God: "Love your neighbor as yourself" (Mark 12:31 NIV). In fact, It is my belief that because so many in our society are not living in the mode of love, that is why there is much hate in our midst.

For example, in the midst of the coronavirus pandemic, those who do not operate in the mode of love invariably will choose to blame others for their suffering. Why? Hate uses the blame game as a way of diverting individual responsibility to others. Not only that, but hate also has its accompanying partners: selfness, greed, and unthankfulness.

Hate Breeds Selfness, Selfness Breeds Greed, and Greed Breeds Unthankfulness

Hate draws in his other partners. In other words, hate breeds selfness, selfness breeds greed, and greed can cause a person to have an attitude of unthankfulness.

But the good news is that love is greater than hate. Those who love God (who is love) become a partaker of His divine love.

Love works no ill toward to his neighbor, and therefore love is the fulfilling of the law (Romans 13:10).

How Should We Say Thanks?

The word *thanks* is a word that we hear less and less in our society today. Essentially, saying thanks is a way of showing appreciation for someone's gift or act of kindness. Today, when we hear the word *thanks*, we often find that it is misused, misguided, and misinterpreted more often than not. The question we need to be ask is, How should we say thanks? Here is what I believe saying thanks means.

1. Saying thanks is saying it with words, but saying thanks is much more than saying it with words.
2. We say thanks when we receive a gift from someone, but saying thanks is much more than receiving a gift.
3. We say thanks by how we use the gift received.
4. In short, thanksgiving is thanksliving.

How we say thanks says a lot about our love for God and each other.

The Rioting and Protesting in the Midst of the Coronavirus Pandemic: What Does It Tells Us about How People Respond in Times of Suffering?

What occurred after the death of George Floyd, who died in police custody in Minneapolis on Monday, May 25, 2020, caused each one of us to question what is happening in our society.

Notice that according to Wikipedia, the data in an April 30, 2020, timeline shows us that the number of COVID-19 deaths in the United States were 60,966, there were 1.04 million conformed cases, and there were 6.25 million total tests completed. Many did not appear to show appreciation for the fact that each one of us could have been counted among the 60,966 deaths. We ought to be thankful that God saw fit to keep us alive.

At the same time, it seems that which happened a few days after 60,966 Americans had lost their lives to the coronavirus highlights is a contradiction in how we should mourn those who have died. We need to take a fresh look at what it means to place value on the sanctity of life and the respect for private and public property.

Look at what happened as a result of George Floyd's death: On May 26, 2020, protesting and rioting began in Minneapolis and subsequently spreading to at least 140 other cities in the United States—even in the midst of a surge in the coronavirus cases and deaths.

I make this observation as a Christian minister of the Gospel being keenly aware of what we are told in the Scripture: Each one of us is born in the image of God, so we are to respect the sanctity of human life (Genesis 1:26–27).

Each individual life is important, and we should mourn the death of even one life. Surely our mourning ought to increase even more when we have lost the lives of thousands of people as a result of the coronavirus or other circumstances.

Here are the questions each one of us need to ask: (1) What does it means when we mourn the death of a person, and even more so when thousands of people (60,966 lives) are lost to the coronavirus pandemic in less than four months? (2) Should the circumstance under which the death(s) occurred make a difference? (3) If we operate in the mode of love, how should our mourning be manifested?

It is my belief that there is a verse in the Gospel of John that helps us understand what is causing people to act in contradicting ways during a time of death and suffering: "The thief comes only to steal and kill and destroy; I have come that they may have life, and have it to the full" (John 10:10 NIV).

First of all, I am very aware that in the context of this passage, Christ is using the shepherd and sheep analogy to convey its meaning. Also, I am very much aware that the meaning is interpreted by different theologians in different ways. However, I am going to use a simple approach to show its full meaning, separating the two phrases into two parts, (*a*) and (*b*).

- Part (a): The thief (Satan) comes only to steal and kill and destroy.
- Part (b): I (God) have come that they may have life, and have it to the full.

In is my belief that part (a) represents Satan and his followers, whereas part (b) represents God and His followers.

With this in mind, let us remember that grief is not meant to be used as a reason to destroy; rather, it is to be used to transform us and draw us closer to God and one another.

Now, with this in mind, each individual needs to ask, "Whose side am I on, God or Satan?" Needless to say, God knows. And also remember that the action we take says a lot about who we are, as well as how and why we demonstrate hate or love.

The good news: It is my observation that the majority of Americans are demonstrating a heartfelt love for each other, helping each other live purposeful lives, and live them more abundantly. Doing so shows what it means to be a real hero.

Chapter 9

What Is the Coronavirus Pandemic Telling Us about the Multilayered Wars We Are Fighting Simultaneously?

Whether we know it or not, in our society, both America and worldwide, we are simultaneously fighting multilayered wars. The number one danger is not knowing we are in a war. The danger in fighting a war is further exacerbated when we do not know the enemy whom we are fighting, and when se we do not really know ourselves.

A quote by Sun Tzu, who was an ancient Chinese general, a military strategist, and the author of *The Art of War*, once wrote,

> If you know the enemy and know yourself, you need not fear the result of a hundred battles. If you know your self but not the enemy, for every victory gained you will also suffer a defeat. If you know neither the enemy nor yourself, you will succumb in every battle.[1]

There is much credence in what the ancient Chinese general said with regard to a war in the physical realm, as well as a war in the spiritual realm.

However, when we talk about a spiritual war, there is another dimension that must be recognized in fighting this type of war, which I will talk about later.

First, however, in staying with the theme of the title of this book, *Searching for Heroes in Life, Vol. 2: What the Coronavirus Pandemic Tells Us about Heroes*, it is important that I focus on the coronavirus as a biological weapon that can be used for the purpose of a biological war by its agent, for good or bad.

We Are in a Biological War

What is a biological war? According to Wikipedia,

> A biological warfare, also known as germ warfare, is the use of biological toxins or infectious agents such as bacteria, viruses, insects, and fungi with the intent to kill, harm, or incapacitate humans, animals or plants as an act of war. Biological or living organism or replicating entities.[2]

Does this definition indicate that the coronavirus is a biological weapon? Yes. You perhaps recall it was said earlier that COVID-19 is a virus, essentially a tiny bit of nucleic acid and protein that needs a host.

Next, we could talk about what agent developed this virus, and where was its origin of discovery. No one can give a definitive answer at this point. Nonetheless, at this juncture, we do know that Wuhan, China, is where it was first discovered.

I do not consider myself a scientist and therefore will not attempt to take part in a blame game as to who is responsible for the coronavirus pandemic spreading throughout the world.

One thing we do know for sure is it is causing much suffering in America and worldwide, in all aspects of our lives. This is a fact that speaks for it itself.

Nevertheless, it is critically important that we recognize we are in a biological war. We are in a war with the coronavirus, that which is an army of invisible soldiers seeking to destroy human beings. Furthermore, by knowing that the coronavirus has an army of invisible soldiers that are led by unknown agents, it is clear we must fight them with our own soldiers.

To better understand how to fight this biological army of biological soldiers and win, it is important that we reemphasize the importance of describing it by the method of *personification.* We must use our imagination to describe it in a way to give it a lifelike, physical form in terms of shape, appearance, and how it functions.

We already know that the enemy soldiers attack the human body from within. They attack the upper respiratory system ("uptown"), and subsequently the lower respiratory system ("downtown"), where it can cause death.

Remember that my primary purpose for writing this book is to show how the coronavirus pandemic is highlighting heroes we have not recognized before. By picturing the coronavirus as an enemy soldier led by enemy agents, we will be able to see the important role our heroic soldiers will play in defeating them.

Furthermore, by knowing that the coronavirus is invisible to the human eye, I will expand on my personification of it as the enemy that we are fighting in biological warfare.

To win this war, we human beings must understand that we must play the role of biological agents in creating visible and invisible soldiers to fight the enemy soldiers both on the outside and on the inside.

To successfully accomplish this task, we need heroes from every walk of life to show up and fight heroically using whatever gifts and talents God has given them.

How Can We Defeat the Coronavirus in This Biological War?

I am sure if we could talk to some of our great American generals, such as Sherman, McArthur, Eisenhower, and Patton, they would unanimously tell us what General Sun Tzu said: (1) To defeat this enemy, we must know the enemy and its capabilities. (2) We must know who we are in terms of capabilities. (3) We must develop and strategize our resources to defeat our enemy. (4) We must develop a plan of attack and execute it in order to defeat the coronavirus, our enemy.

Last but not least, we must not forget a very important question one must ask before one fights in a war: Do I have the will to fight? The answer must be yes.

What We Know about the Coronavirus, the Enemy Soldier

It has already been established that the coronavirus is invisible to the naked eye. With this in mind, let me refresh our memory as we use our imagination and personify it, to give it a lifelike form that can help us to better focus on the task at hand.

1. It is spherical in shape, and its outer skin is membranous. Its roundness gives it the ability to change in any direction while moving with equal speed.
2. We cannot say for sure, and because we do not have a full understanding of the nature of color in the microscopic world, we cannot give it a definitive color. However, for the sake of personification, we will describe it as a mixture of scary red, icky green, sickly yellow, and many colors in between.
3. The spiky, spongy feet, which we will say are red, are equally spaced in a triangular pattern on the entire spherical outer surface. This would seemingly allow it to

land on its involuntary host (object) with any part of its outer surface.

4. COVID-19 is a virus that essentially contains a combination of nucleic acids and proteins that need a living host to do damage. The fact is the virus hitchhikes onto the hosts without its permission.

5. The virus can spread from person to person within six feet through droplets that are produced when an infected person coughs or sneezes.

6. It also is possible for the enemy virus to remain on a surface or object, and to be transferred by touch and enter the body though the mouth, nose, or eyes.

7. Once inside the body, it first attacks the upper respiratory tract, which I will call "uptown."

8. In extreme cases, it travels to the lower respiratory tract, which I will call "downtown."

9. Also, it is important to remember that once inside the human body, it attacks the immune system.

10. In addition, once inside the human body, it can replicate itself. This means it can replicate itself by mutating into variants of its original form, and it can possibly become deadlier.

May we never forget that the enemy soldiers does not ask for our permission and they can attack us by the millions, by the billions, and by the trillions at an exponential rate.

Question is, Who will stop them? It is my belief that God can stop the coronavirus enemy at any time, and at other times He comes to humans through humans, in that He can use humans as his instrument to defeat this enemy soldier.

We can take comfort in knowing that when God is with us, we are more than those against us. What role must we take in order to defect this enemy?

What Task or Role Must Humans Play in Defeating the Enemy Soldier, the Coronavirus?

We learned earlier from an ancient Chinese general, general Sun Tzu, that in order to win a war, we must know our enemy, and we must know ourselves.

I reiterate: We must factor in another critical understanding of what we need to win a war. We must have a will to win. And our will to win must be guided by what God tells us in Proverbs:

> Trust in the LORD with all your heart, and lean
> not on your own understanding; in all your ways
> acknowledge Him, and He will direct your paths.
> (Proverbs 3:5–6 KJV).

In other words, when God, the one who has never lost a battle, is on our side, we will never lose a battle. With this in mind, let's get busy and defeat the invisible enemy soldiers, the coronavirus.

Our first order of day is to pray to God to defeat this coronavirus enemy. And as He uses men and women, boys and girls, as heroic soldiers, we can be confident that we will be victorious. When we allow this to happen, we will discover that God can use this war to bring out heroic deeds in us when we allow Him to use us as His soldiers.

Are You Ready to Be a Hero in This War?

Now that we know more about the enemy soldier, the coronavirus, and what it is capable of doing, and most of all, now we know that with God on our side, victory awaits us ahead. The good news is that we have already discovered we must make every effort to develop weapons that will defeat this invisible, biological enemy soldier, the coronavirus.

No one is exempt from this war. Each one must understand that this is not a voluntary war; rather, it is a nonvoluntary war, and every man, woman, boy, and girl must assume their post and be vigilant. As you do so, remember heroes are not born heroes; rather, heroes are made.

We Must Be Able to Attack Our Enemy, Both on the Outside and Inside of Our Bodies, and Our Tactics Must Be Both Defensive and Offensive

The good news is that we have already learned a lot about how to fight the biological enemy soldiers. For example, we have developed weapons such as antibacterial sprays to attack the enemy on the outside of the human body. We have developed face masks and other face coverings, and even body coverings, to combat and defend from the outside of the body. However, It is critical that we develop weapons to use on the inside of the human body to defect the coronavirus. What invisible weapons have we developed so far?

Further good news: We have already developed vaccine weapons that can be injected into the human body to defeat the invisible enemy that has entered the inside of the body and seeks to do damage to the upper respiratory system (uptown), and subsequently the lower respiratory system (downtown).

The knowledge we have gained thus far about how the enemy operates in this biological war has taught us that we must go where the enemy is in order to defeat it. Thus, because we know the enemy does its real damage after it enters the human body, we must likewise send our invisible soldiers into the human body to ultimately defeat the enemy in the respiratory system.

To put it another way, in order to defeat the coronavirus enemy, our soldiers, the coronavirus vaccines and other prescribed therapeutic medicines, must be able to go uptown or downtown, wherever the enemy goes.

Let's look at what has been done to accomplish this task thus far.

Again, Let Us Be Thankful for What Has Already Been Done in Fighting This Biological War against the Coronavirus

It is my belief that to know where you are, you must first know where you came from, and in order to know where you are going, you must know where you are.

With respect to where we have come from as a result of Operation Warp Speed, we were successful in developing three coronavirus vaccines in less than nine months. In addition, America has been successful in building thousands of life-support incubators, coronavirus test equipment, and numerous other medical protective items, along with the discoveries of other therapeutic medicines that have been approved for emergency use by the FDA. America has come a long way in preparing to defeat the coronavirus.

Again, let us give credit to President Trump's administration, scientists, private sectors, pharmaceutical companies, and government agencies, and millions of other Americans from all walks of life who have stepped up to the plate and delivered in heroic ways.

Let us thank each other for our efforts this far. However, let us not take our eyes of the task ahead. For we are already discovering that the coronavirus is replicating itself in the form of mutational variants that can present long-lasting challenges for us in the future.

But know this one thing: With God on our side, and with us working together for the common good of all, we can be more than conquerors through God, who loves us (Romans 8:37).

Where to from Here?

Now that we have been blessed with the ability to combat and defeat this enemy, the coronavirus, where do we go from here?

First, those of us whom God has thus far allowed to survive the coronavirus pandemic should take pause and thank God and all our heroes along the way.

Second, may we never forget that the coronavirus is able to replicate itself and therefore change into variants of another variant. That is a reminder to us that we must continue to operate in the mode of eternal vigilance in order to defeat the coronavirus and the variants that may occur in the future.

Finally, we must never forget that God is still in control, and whatever He allows to happen in our lives, it is to ultimately work for good (Romans 8:28).

Meanwhile, may we use the coronavirus pandemic as a reminder of the sense of urgency in our lives, and the fact that life is short in terms of eternity. Now is the time to truly think about our eternal well-being and the importance of having a true relationship to God. In fact, this leads me to talk about another war: spiritual warfare.

Unknown to Many, We Are in a Spiritual War

In a world that often seems to grow gray and dim under the weight of trouble and discord, I could easily talk about other wars in our midst, such as political wars, ideology wars, terrorist wars, racial wars, and cold wars, that highlight heroes, or even non-heroes. However, it is my belief that the war that helps explain all other wars is the *spiritual warfare* that is unknown to many.

The mistake that many make, especially in our Western culture, is that we attempt to draw a line, albeit it an invisible one, between the natural realm and the spiritual realm. But the truth is God created both, the natural realm and the spiritual realm.

Again, remember that God created the whole world (universe) and everything therein (Acts 17:24). This means He created both the spiritual and natural realms. And He controls both.

We must remember that because God transcends both the natural and spiritual realms, He is able to use the spiritual realm to permeate and operate in the natural realm to carry out His purpose.

We have a tendency, as many scientists do, to determine reality by using only empirical evidence. Humans too often try to define reality through our five senses, sight, sound, smell, taste, and touch. But God will have us to know that the reality of existence is much more than the physical aspects of existence. We must also remember we are created with body, soul, and spirit. And we relate to God through our human spirit.

This is where Satan comes in. Remember: Satan and his evil angels are already defeated foes, with no chance of redemption. So do not be surprised that his job is to keep as many of us as he can from having a relationship with God.

How to Defeat Satan and Evil in Spiritual Warfare

We are in a spiritual warfare as proclaimed in Ephesians 6:

> Finally be strong in the Lord and in His mighty power. Put on the full armor of God so that you can take your stand against the devil's scheme. For Our struggle is not against flesh and blood, but against the rulers, against the authorities, against the powers of this dark world and against the spiritual forces of evil in heavenly realms. Therefore put on the whole armor of God, so that when the day of evil comes, you may be able stand your ground … And pray in the Spirit on all

occasions with all kinds of prayers and requests. (Ephesians 6:10–13, 18 NIV)

But the big question remains: Whose side are you on? The Scripture reminds us as Paul speaks through the inspiration of the Spirit of God: "Without faith it is impossible to please God: because anyone who comes to Him must believe that He exists, and that He rewards those who earnestly seek Him" (Hebrews 11:6 NIV).

So I say to all the wonderful heroes in our midst: When you feel like fear is overcoming you, you are discouraged, you are experiencing a sense of hopelessness, and you are worried about what tomorrow may bring, remember what God says as He speaks through Apostle Paul in 2 Corinthians 4:8–9 (KJV), "We are troubled on every side, yet not distressed; We are perplexed, but not in despair; persecuted, but not forsaken; castdown, but not destroyed."

And listen as God speaks through Apostle John: "In the world you shall have tribulation (trouble), but be of good cheer, I have overcome the world" (John 16:33 KJV).

When we have the right relationship with God, and when we believe that He is faithful and able to keep His promises, we can take comfort in knowing that God has already overcome the world and that victory awaits us.

Chapter 10

The Importance of Knowing That We Are in a Spiritual War

Knowing that we are in a biological war and a spiritual war, what must we do as we wait for the ultimate victory? Elisha gives the answer. It is the story of Elisa and the chariots of fire that reminds us God can give us the spiritual eye to see Him in action.

Can You See the Chariots of Fire?

When I think about the chariots of fire, I am reminded of what happened when Elisa, the prophet of God, was surrounded by the king of Aram in the days of Ancient Israel.

> King Aram sent his army out to capture Elisha in a place called Dothan. King Aram had ordered his officers to send his horses and chariot by night and surround the city where Elisha and his men were encamped.
>
> Early the next morning one of the servants of Elisha got up and went out in the open. At first

he noticed the beauty of the sun rays cascading over the mountain tops.

But something else caught his eye! As he looked out he saw a sight that shooked him to his bones. He saw that an army with horses and chariots had surrounded the city. He looked to the North, he looked to the East, he looked to the South, and he looked to the West, and he saw the enemy all around them making ready for attack.

And as fast as his feet would carry him, he ran to where Elisha was sitting and said: "Oh, my lord, what shall we do?" The servant asked.

"Do not be afraid," the prophet Elisha answered. "Those who are with us are more than those who are against us."

And then Elisha did something we all should do when we are surrounded and hounded by the enemy; and it seems like there is no way out:

Elisha bowed down on his knees and looked towards heaven from which his help comes. Elisha prayed: "O LORD, open his eyes so he may see." (2 Kings 6:8–17 KJV)

Oh, for a Spiritual Eye to See

Then the LORD opened the servant's eyes, and he looked and saw the hills full of horses, pawing, dancing and prancing in place, as the swords of the angelic riders were glittering and glistening

in the light of God's glory, as they set on their
chariots of fire that surrounded all around Elisha
(2 Kings 6:17 KJV).

This story is a reminder to us today, as we endure the coronavirus
enemy soldiers, that when in the midst of trials and tribulations,
with hardships, hopelessness, fear, and trouble all around, may
we do as Elisha did for his servant. Pray that God will give us a
spiritual eye to see God's chariot of fire protecting us from all
around.

God is looking for heroes like Elisha today who are connected
to God. God is looking for people in every walk of life to ask God
to use them to be a hero for God and humankind. When we allow
this to happen, we will know that God is in control and that His
love will never fail. This is what we can learn from Elisha.

Now, look at what we have learned thus far from those who
have walked with us during the coronavirus pandemic and what
it says about each one of them.

Chapter 11

What Are We Learning from Our Journey through the Coronavirus Pandemic This Far?

What have we learned from our own journey through the coronavirus pandemic this far? It is a personal question that each one of us needs to ask of ourselves. In answering this personal question, I am speaking about that which I have experienced, that which I have seen with my own eyes, and that which I have heard with my own ears, both in the natural and spiritual realms.

The chariots of fire story as told about Elisha and his servant is a picture of what I have experienced during the coronavirus pandemic, in terms of how a person's spiritual discernment is tested during the times our faith.

Here is what I have found: There those like Elisha's servant who feared because he was looking at his circumstances through his physical eyes, and there are those like Elisha who, because of his close relationship with God, had the ability to see spiritually.

Notice what happened when Elisha asked God to give his servant the spiritual ability to see. God answered Elisha prayer. He gave Elisha's servant the ability to see spiritually too.

The good news is I have seen this scenario play out in our midst. I have seen men and women, boys and girls, praying for one another. I have seen the spiritually strong help the spiritually weak. I have seen the physically strong help the physically weak. It is a reminder that when people from all walks of life join together with one accord, we can be heroes for God and each other.

However, I would be remiss if I did not remind you that I also see much hate prevailing in our midst. We have endured suffering, pain, and hardship in the midst of the coronavirus pandemic. And likewise, as we are experiencing the insurgency of variants, the blame game and the hate game seem to have intensified. But here is what I do know: love is greater than hate.

> So we have come to know and believe the love that God has for us, God is love, whoever abides in love abides in God, and God abides him. (1 John 4:16 KJV)

God's Love Is Unconditional and Can Heal All Our Brokenness, Both in the Natural Realm and the Spiritual Realm

In times like these, may we know that we can depend on God's unconditional love. We must press on with the attitude and faith that Apostle Paul had during his earthly journey:

> We are troubled on every side, yet not distressed; We are perplexed, but not in despair; persecuted, but not forsaken; cast down but not destroyed. (2 Corinthians 4:8–9 KJV)

And may we claim what Apostle Paul says in Romans 8:

> Who shall separate us from the love of Christ? Shall tribulation, or distress, or persecution, or famine, or nakedness, or peril, or sword.?

Nay in all these things we are more than conquerors through Him that loved us.

For I am persuaded, that neither death, nor life,nor angels, nor principalities, nor powers, nor things present, nor things to come,

Nor height, nor depth, nor any other creature, shall be able to separate us from the love of God, which is in Christ Jesus our Lord. (Romans 8: 35, 37–39 KJV)

May we always be thankful for the immeasurable knowledge we have gained in our efforts to eradicate the coronavirus and its variants. These events have taught us to expect the best but be prepared for what is to come, both in the spiritual and natural realms.

It is my hope that the knowledge and experience we have gained has accelerated our emergency preparation and readiness to combat the coronavirus and its variants, as well as other emergencies, in the days ahead. May we not forget to thank God for sparing us the opportunity to live another day.

And last but not least, may we be thankful for all the newfound heroes, highlighted by the coronavirus pandemic. To all our heroes: As you operate in the mode of love, in the midst of the coronavirus pandemic, and in whatever circumstance you may face in the days to come, remember to brighten up the corner where you are. May you continue to show gratitude for heroes in our midst, heroes from every walk of life, both seen and unseen.

Finally, may you continue to be a hero for God and others, for your labor is not in vain.

—Charles Brookins Taylor, Sr.

Notes

Chapter 1: Using the Tool of Repetition

1   Dr. Saul McLeod, updated December 29, 2020, accessed, November 11, 2021, https://www.simplypsychology.org/maslow.html

Chapter 3: The Coronavirus Pandemic Appearance on the Scene Has Caused Dramatic Changes Worldwide

1   World Health Organization, April 12, 2020, https://www.who.int.doc.20200423-sitrep-94-civid-10.
2   CDC Museum, "COVID-19 Timeline," December 12, 2020, https://www.cdc.gov/museum.timeline.Covid19.

Chapter 4: What Sets the Coronavirus Pandemic apart From Prior Pandemics, Plagues, and Other Disasters

1   Ellie Riley, October 21,2021, accessed November 30, 2021, https://www.Goodrx.com/conditions/covid-19/what-does-pandemic means-with-examples-vs-epidemic
2   "Coronavirus Transmission," October 27, 2020, https://www.webmed.com/lung/coronavirus-transmission-overview-print+true.
3   Heather Strah, July 7, 2020, accessed October 30, 2020, https://www.nebraskamed.com/heather-m-strah; Heather Strah, https://www.nebraska. com/COVID-19/what-the-Coronavirus-does-to-your-body.
4   March 20, 2020, https://dictionary.com/e/is-the-coronavirus-a-plaque/.
5   "Natural Disaster," Wikipedia, accessed December 29, 2020, en.widipedia.org/wiki/natural-disaster.

6   "Case Study in Psychology, Wikipedia, accessed November 17, 2020, https://en.wikipedia.org/wiki/Case-study.

7   Natural Resources, September 8, 2020, https://toppr.com.

8   August 11, 2020, https://worldmeter.info.world population.

9   May 20, 2021, https//www.worldmeter.info.us-population

10 February 20, 2020, https://theglobaleconomy.com/ranking/labor-force-participation/.

11 Rakesh Kochar, June 11, 2020, accessed May 26, 2021, https://pewresearch.org/fact-tank/2020/11/unemployment-rose-higher-in-three-months-of-covid-19-than-it- did-in-two-years-of-the-great-recess...

Chapter 5: Ways We Are Responding

1   "Operation Warp Speed," Wikipedia, accessed June 5, 2020, https://wikipedia.org/wiki/ Operation-Warp-Speed.

2   Ibid.

3   Ibid.

4   July 7, 2021, https://www.fda-gov. emergency-use-authorization-covid- 19 vacines.

Chapter 6: Observing and Dialoguing with Heroes in Our Midst

1   August 16, 2020, https://academictherapycenter.com/about/.

Chapter 9: What Is the Coronavirus Pandemic Telling Us about the Multilayered Wars We Are Fighting Simultaneously?

1   "The Art of War," Wikipedia, accessed November 11, 2020, https://en.wikipedia.org/wiki/The-Art-of-War.

2   "Biological Warfare," Wikipedia, accessed November 10, 2020, https://en.wikipedia/en.widipedia.org/wiki/biological-warfare.

Printed in the United States
by Baker & Taylor Publisher Services